Tim Skelly

D1710895

Return to Meaning

Return to Meaning

A Social Science with Something to Say

Mats Alvesson, Yiannis Gabriel, and Roland Paulsen

OXFORD
UNIVERSITY PRESS

OXFORD
UNIVERSITY PRESS

Great Clarendon Street, Oxford, OX2 6DP,
United Kingdom

Oxford University Press is a department of the University of Oxford.
It furthers the University's objective of excellence in research, scholarship,
and education by publishing worldwide. Oxford is a registered trade mark of
Oxford University Press in the UK and in certain other countries

First Edition published in 2017
Impression: 1

Published in the United States of America by Oxford University Press
198 Madison Avenue, New York, NY 10016, United States of America

British Library Cataloguing in Publication Data
Data available

Library of Congress Control Number: 2016959791

ISBN 978–0–19–878709–9

Printed and bound by
CPI Group (UK) Ltd, Croydon, CR0 4YY

Acknowledgements

We would like to acknowledge the help and encouragement of numerous colleagues who read the manuscript and gave us their views at different stages of its development, held many discussions with us, and participated in a workshop debating some of the main themes of this book. These include Dan Kärreman, Mats Benner, Tony Huzzard, Sonja Opper, Rajani Naidoo, Jurgen Enders, Richard Swedberg, and many others. We would like to express our special thanks and gratitude to David Musson, a great believer in the core arguments of this book, who encouraged us since its earliest inception and provided a constant source of inspiration and support.

Mats Alvesson
Yiannis Gabriel
Roland Paulsen

Contents

Part I
Loss of Meaning

1

The Problem

So Much Noise, So Little to Say

In 1965, John Williams published the novel *Stoner* which follows the life of William Stoner, a remarkably unremarkable professor at a Midwestern university. The book received good reviews and sold around 2,000 copies before it went out of print a year later. In 2011, it received an unexpected renaissance and within a couple of years it sold more than 200,000 copies in the UK alone while being rapidly translated into twenty-one languages. Apparently, something about the farm boy from Missouri who, after 'falling in love' with Shakespeare's *Sonnet 73*, goes on to become an assistant professor, struck a chord with readers in the 2010s. It is hard to explain why. The central character leads a quite uneventful life. At least on the surface, there is not that much to celebrate. He lives through most of his life with a sadistic and manipulative wife who he cannot leave. For decades he has to subordinate himself to an even more sadistic dean who spares no effort to destroy his career. He has a daughter who momentarily lights up his life only to slowly fade away into alcoholism. He has a brief affair—and then he dies of cancer.

Perhaps these commonplace sorrows still live up to the public image of what it means to be an academic. Perhaps the public enjoys reading about the forgotten lives circulating in those lofty university buildings. Yet, there is one point at which the life of Stoner strongly differs from the life of today's academics. Although he sometimes ponders whether he should write something new, a book perhaps, the totality of his academic production amounts to one single item: his PhD thesis. While spending the entirety of his adult life in academia, he never writes anything more than that. At the end of the novel, while lying on his deathbed, he finds the thesis at his bedside table. Letting his fingers riffle through the pages, he feels 'a tingling, as if those pages were alive', and with the sense of having left more to the world than an estranged wife, daughter, and mistress, he dies in sublime reconciliation with his life while the book slips out of his hands and falls to the floor (Williams, 1965, p. 227).

If contentment with having written a thesis and nothing else was mysterious in the 1960s, it would appear almost inconceivable to present-day academics. Today, 'publish or perish' is but a euphemism of academic life; in James Hynes' (1998) words, 'publish *and* perish' appears closer to reality. When Williams (who was also assistant professor at the University of Denver) wrote *Stoner* in the 1960s, 40 per cent of those working in American four-year higher educational colleges had had no publications over their entire careers. Thirty years later, that proportion had shrunk to 18 per cent (Schuster & Finkelstein, 2008, p. 474). Likewise, in the 1960s, only 20 per cent of this professional group agreed that 'tenure is difficult to attain without research/publications'. Thirty years later, 64 per cent agreed (Schuster & Finkelstein, 2008, p. 490).

Since the 1990s, the amount of academic publishing has grown immensely, even allowing for the rapid increase in the number of academics. According to UNESCO's Institute for Statistics, the number of tertiary education teachers in the USA rose from just under one million in 1999 to nearly 1.6 million in 2013. Similar rises have been taking place elsewhere, as higher education has become a global industry. What has outpaced even the rise of academics has been the rise in academic publications. It is estimated that in 1996 over one million academic articles were published, whereas in 2009 the number had increased to a million and a half (about one new article every twenty-two seconds). Between 200 and 300 new scientific journals are published each year, amounting to a total of more than 12,000 (Campbell & Meadows, 2011; STM, 2010) without including countless e-journals and other online publications.

Given this explosion of research 'outputs', it comes as no surprise that many scholars have begun to question its purpose and its consequences. Some have suggested that the current overproduction of academic papers is straining the peer-review system and leading to a decline in standards (e.g. Harley & Acord, 2011). Others question why it is now seen as necessary for those who teach in universities to publish everything they think or say in the classroom (e.g. Parker, 2013). This critique is concerned with intrinsic issues regarding the value and meaning of scientific research per se as well as extrinsic issues regarding its value and meaning to society at large. Our book develops this critique before trying to propose some constructive ways forward. We argue that we are currently witnessing not merely a decline in the quality of scientific research, but a proliferation of meaningless research of no value to society and of only modest value to its authors—apart from in the context of securing employment and promotion. The explosion of published outputs, at least in social science, creates a noisy, cluttered environment which makes meaningful research difficult to identify and develop as well as rare, as different voices compete to capture the limelight even briefly. More impressive contributions from some years ago are easily neglected, as the premium now is to write and publish, not to read and learn. The result is a widespread cynicism among academics on the merits of academic research, sometimes including their own. Publishing comes to be seen as a game of hit and miss, of targets and rankings, crucial for the fashioning of academic careers and institutional prestige but devoid of intrinsic meaning and value, and of no wider social uses whatsoever. This is what we view as the rise of nonsense in academic research. We believe that this represents a serious social *problem*. It undermines the very point of social science—the target of this book, even though most of what we are saying is probably relevant for all areas of science.

Throughout this book, we unashamedly use the word 'problem' to denote the extensive failure of social science to address the burning issues of our time, the anxiety and frustration engendered by the proliferation of esoteric and meaningless texts, and the resulting instrumental and cynical attitudes about academic work both inside and outside universities. The problem is far from 'academic'. It affects many areas of social and political life, entailing extensive waste of resources and inflated student fees as well as costs to taxpayers. Resources allocated to social research often are at the expense of teaching. Instead of providing support for teaching, a strong emphasis on research may easily encourage academics to narrowly focus on their sub-specialities and to concentrate on reading recently published articles rather than more significant but older books—which are more valuable for genuine scholarship. Most seriously, however, the problem results in an enduring disconnection between the generation and dissemination of knowledge in social science and the pressing needs of a society facing major challenges.

Although this book focusses on social science, and to some extent our own specialities of organization studies and the sociology of work, we see many connections to other areas and believe that much of what we say is relevant across academia. Critiques similar to ours are increasingly heard in other disciplines than the social sciences (for example, Edwards & Siddharta, 2016).

The Problem with Nonsense

Nothing illustrates better the rise of nonsense research than three publishing experiments that revealed how easy it is for literal nonsense to appear in reputable academic publications. The first experiment was performed by the physicist Alan Sokal who in 1996 wrote an article describing how he had managed to publish a paper in the journal *Social Text*. *Social Text* was no run-of-the-mill journal. It boasted well-known academics on its editorial staff and was widely read in the field of cultural studies. Sokal had submitted an article in which he used quantum physics and obscure mathematical formulae to express support for the rationales of, among others, Jacques Lacan and Jacques Derrida. The article was well written and made a serious impression. There was only one problem: it contained no substantial argument. Sokal had submitted it to see if a journal respected in its field would accept the text if it sounded good and was in line with the political convictions of the editors. The answer was an unequivocal yes (Sokal, 1996).

The Sokal affair gave rise to a debate on whether postmodern social science could be considered scientific. Instead of discussing its wider ramifications for every discipline, the debate centred on a specific discipline. In 2013, however, the biologist John Bohannon did a similar experiment in biology, submitting an essay of poorly concealed nonsense. According to Bohannon, '[a]ny reviewer with more than a high-school knowledge of chemistry and the ability to understand a basic data plot should have spotted the paper's short-comings immediately. Its experiments are so hopelessly flawed that the results are meaningless' (Bohannon, 2013, p. 66). More than half of the 304 scientific journals to which he sent the essay agreed to publish it, including several journals published by Sage, Elsevier, Wolter Kluwer, and other publishing giants. Now natural science was also being questioned.

Things would become even more spectacular when three postgraduate students from the Massachusetts Institute of Technology decided to expose their colleagues. The postgraduate students developed a program called SCIgen which generated so-called 'gobbledegook articles' containing graphs and diagrams as well as barely readable sentences randomly generated by the program and thus devoid of meaning. An article produced in this way, 'Rooter: a methodology for the typical unification of access points and redundancy' was accepted for a scientific conference on systems science, cybernetics, and informatics and the hoax was later revealed in *Nature* (Ball, 2005). Almost ten years after that, a new discovery was made giving the SCIgen-experiment new relevance. In 2005, SCIgen had become generally accessible on the Internet, allowing anyone to create nonsensical articles. In 2013, a French programmer developed a software program to discover SCIgen-genererated articles. After scanning articles on computer science published between 2008 and 2013, he found that over 120 were pure gobbledegook. Sixteen of these had been published by Springer and had to be hastily withdrawn (Noorden, 2014).

These affairs confirm a feeling that has now become difficult for researchers to avoid: the feeling that at least a substantial part of what is written and published in the name of science is nonsense, meaningless, or in other ways deeply problematic. Human nonsense usually has a syntax that is more or less comprehensible and sometimes also contains grains of non-nonsense. But what was now being revealed was that the scientific community had developed a major inability to expose *utter* nonsense—nonsense which would never be tolerated in a daily newspaper, a gossip magazine, or even in a poorly-written children's book. It could quite simply not see that the emperor's new clothes were fake.

As social scientists, we often get a strong feeling of 'semi-nonsense' in what we read. Behind abstract and pretentious academic jargon and the use of signifiers indicating that the author is dealing with important topics—strategic leadership, knowledge management, sociomateriality, intertextuality—complicated statistical materials or a profusion of interview statements (frequently removed from their social context), we regularly feel that there is not much of substance in what we read. Alternatively, we have the feeling of reading pretentious articles where commonsense is camouflaged, or variations on long-standing or even long-discredited themes. Claiming an original and unique 'contribution' is currently de rigueur in every research publication, yet, this usually amounts to trivial additions to small outposts of literature only meaningful to tiny research microtribes. One may rightly ask whether there is any value in the average additional article on topics like neo-institutional theory, postfeminist discourse, or managerial leadership, after thousands of studies in these areas. An expert in a specific sub-subfield may find the details and incremental 'contributions' of such articles meaningful, but scholars with a broader range of interests and a non-nerdish mentality may have trouble appreciating their value or originality. The proliferation of texts within sub- or sub-sub-specialisms has led to the fragmentation of scholarly communities into microtribes with highly parochial interests and concerns, safeguarding these interests from the attention of other microtribes, carefully controlling entry into their domains only to those who master its conventions, rituals, and jargons. Some microtribes are more successful than others, but the boundaries between them result not only in alienation and frustration, but in missed opportunities for original and creative work.

One of the indicators of scientific merit that has gained in popularity is citability—this is especially so in the last twenty years when the references of each and every publication are meticulously recorded and counted by agencies like Scopus or World of Science. This led to a mushrooming of citations (and self-citations), often of articles whose authors act as manuscript reviewers or editors. Citability by itself is an unreliable measure, given that some valuable articles may lie unnoticed and uncited in the noisy environment they inhabit. Yet, even by this criterion, the human sciences are not doing particularly well with some 90 per cent of all published articles remaining uncited within a two-year window. Within a five-year citation window, 84 per cent stay uncited in Thomson Reuters' Web of Science. In the social science as a whole, around half of all published articles remain uncited in a two-year citation window that determines a journal's impact factor. Within a five-year window, 32 per cent go uncited. This compares with no more than 12 per cent uncited articles in medicine (Larivière, Gingras, & Archambault, 2009). Even 'high-impact' journals in social science can suffer from a crowd of 'lonely papers' (Prichard, 2013).

'Qualitative' indicators reinforce this rather gloomy picture. A common response when reviewing papers is a deep sigh and the reflection: what is the point of all this? 'It is easy to become cynical' is a repeated remark in social science conferences, one that captures the prevailing mood of pointlessness, lack of social relevance, and dearth of interesting presentations that make a difference to scholarship outside the tribe or to society at large (Alvesson & Sandberg, 2013). Even the editors of prestigious journals, rejecting 95 per cent or so of all submissions, are now regularly complaining about their inability to publish studies that go beyond the incremental. Reflecting back on the years since launching what quickly turned out to be a high-impact journal, *Organization Science*, Daft and Lewin (2008, p. 177) conceded that their original mission to reorient organizational 'research away from incremental, footnote-on-footnote research as the norm for the field' (Daft & Lewin, 1990, p. 1) had not been realized. They re-emphasized the need not to prioritize incremental research but, instead, 'new theories and ways of thinking about organizations' (Daft & Lewin, 2008, p. 182). Similarly, the outgoing editors of another leading journal—based on a review of more than 3,000 manuscripts during their six years in office (2003–08)—noted in their concluding editorial that while submissions had increased heavily 'it is hard to conclude that this has been accompanied by a corresponding increase in papers that add significantly to the discipline. More is being produced but the big impact papers remain elusive ... ' (Clark & Wright, 2009, p. 6). Equally, as the editors of *Academy of Management Journal* (*AMJ*), another high-profiled journal, Bartunek et al. (2006, p. 9) argued that while the journal is publishing 'technically competent research that simultaneously contributes to theory ... [it is] desirable to raise the proportion of articles published in *AMJ* that are regarded as important, competently executed, and *really interesting*'. A later editor of the same journal complained that 'like black cats in coal cellars, published studies are increasingly indistinguishable from previous ones, and the contexts in which these theories are tested or developed tend to fade into irrelevance' (George, 2014, p. 1).

These testimonies reinforce the impression that the explosion of research publications very seldom results in something original and profoundly insightful. This is confirmed by the views of many academics themselves, typified by a lecturer interviewed by Knights and Clarke:

> Our research exists in a very selfish domain ... half the crap that you read in some of the four-star journals has absolutely no benefit or carries no significance for virtually anything, anywhere for anybody other than the author.   (Lecturer, cited in Knights & Clarke, 2014, p. 345)

Given the huge rise of researchers and research papers in recent decades, one may justifiably say that 'never before in the history of humanity have so many written so much while having so little to say to so few'. When one of us used this expression at a conference, the audience of some 400 people applauded spontaneously, apparently confirming the impression.

'Nonsense' may be a strong word. We use it broadly to denote theoretical knowledge that fulfils all the formal criteria for 'good, publishable research' and is thus dressed in academic respectability, without offering any new insights or empirical findings that have a wider social relevance or meaning, or are capable of adding positively to society. The writing, reviewing, editing, and publishing of such nonsense accounts for the view of academics retreating into ingrown sectarianisms (Burawoy, 2005, p. 17) becoming 'models of moral indifference and examples of what it means to disconnect themselves from public life' and 'making almost no connections to audiences outside of the academy' (Giroux, 2006, p. 64).

This brings us to the extrinsic part of the critique and more precisely to the question of what science can offer to society. As researchers, often on the watch for funding and eager to jump on fashionable topics of inquiry, we tend to ask the opposite question: what can society offer to science? Too often the relevance of our work is but merely concocted in hindsight. Or worse; thinking about it risks instrumentalizing science and restricting its autonomy. As scientists, we vehemently defend our right to decide what areas of knowledge we pursue, concerned that science should not be subordinated to the interests of governments, businesses, or social movements. The argument we put forward in this book, however, is that as researchers we have a responsibility to establish the meaning of what we do and demonstrate its social value beyond our narrow self- or tribal-interests. This is an area in which natural scientists and social scientists find themselves facing different challenges. Much research in natural science (including engineering and medicine) may be unintelligible to the laity but can be shown to have value to society. Most people would agree that medical, scientific, and technological breakthroughs engender at least the potential for enhancing human life, widening the horizons of knowledge, and reducing unnecessary pain and suffering. Even small advances in natural science can cross-fertilize with others to generate innovations and products with significant social and economic consequences.

The consequences of social science research, however, are not so straightforward. The object of social science—people and society—is a contingent entity; it is in constant change, a change in which ideas and practices resulting from social science itself play a part. From the cognitive workings of the human psyche to the fluctuations of the global economy, few would be ready to formulate general laws of the same universal character and predictive power of natural laws. Therefore, social science is not cumulative even in the limited sense that natural science is. There is great cultural variation and historical change. We may of course aim to add to our knowledge of psychological, organizational, or cultural processes for instance, but although some social scientists would argue otherwise (most notoriously August Comte, see Marcuse, 1955; Turner, 2007 for critique) we cannot reach confident generalizations that apply in every context and every situation. It is not possible, for example, to figure out how all the parts constituting a workplace should behave in order to work optimally in the same way as we can say how the parts of the human knee or wetland ecosystems should behave. A workplace is immensely complicated and will change over time, with endless contingencies and a variety of internal dynamics, all related to the social constructions of goals, technologies, internal and external relations, rules, authority beliefs, gender, class, age, ethnicity issues, management structures, changing work ideologies, mass media coverage, etc. And social science knowledge will be an intrinsic part of workplace functioning, affected by social technologies partly emerging from psychological, economical, sociological, and management theories on work and organization.

Unlike natural phenomena, human institutions, practices, and actions are imbued with meaning, their subjects sentient beings with motives, emotions, and aspirations that can be surprising, mysterious, or perverse. Understanding human actions calls for different types of explanation and interpretation than that from the behaviours of molecules, magnets, or machines. Social science is, as Giddens (1982) phrased it, about double hermeneutics; interpreting researchers study interpreting subjects. In carrying out social research, we are potentially capable of changing the object of our investigation, for better or worse. We can, for example, enable a poorly performing hospital to improve the service it offers to its community, or a dormant innovation to be put into effect in enhancing the lives of different people. Conversely, we can seriously mislead or muddle policy-makers with ill thought out theories, buzzwords, and faddish practices that cause unnecessary upheaval and suffering. Or we can seduce managers into believing that they can be fantastic leaders and change uncertain, lazy, anxious, and incompetent subordinates into enthusiastic, engaged, self-conscious, and skilled followers. Unfortunately, the current profusion of research publications makes it increasingly difficult to tell the wheat from the chaff, to identify any potential uses and abuses of social science, and to evaluate the merits of different claims.

Social science also strikes a different relation with its readership. Most texts in the natural sciences address a narrow circle of scientific experts able to judge their merits and applications. The wider public and policy-makers are not in a position to assess the scientific claims of this research but can debate and implement its applications. A new medical treatment or a new type of security camera may be based on scientific innovations only comprehensible to a small group of scientists—whether the treatment or the security camera should be used in particular situations on grounds of costs, ethics, side effects, or whatever, can then be debated by the public and their representatives. The situation with social science is different. Without a broader readership, social science can rarely have an effect, in particular if there is no policy implication that can be directly implemented. Policy-makers and politicians but also consultants, journalists, social commentators, and other opinion-shapers are unlikely to pick up and debate findings from a social science that is buried in obscure journals that very few people can access and even fewer read. The public itself is often potentially in a position to judge many of the insights generated by social science research but cannot do so without the ability to access it. This calls for social research to be widely read and for the texts to have something new and meaningful to say—to appeal to and do something with the reader. In other words, social science texts need to be performative to be 'fully' meaningful. Published research findings should be written, and expressed, in ways that make them inviting to read.

In light of this, it is not surprising that largely meaningless and esoteric texts of social research languish unread, unloved, and unappreciated, constituting little more than noise for researchers. As we shall see, this has extensive practical implications. Meaningless and esoteric texts have the ability to clutter out and silence valuable research that might usefully guide policy or avert different instances of malpractice and mismanagement. Social scientists have often found themselves acting as Cassandras—calling attention to serious social problems (obesity, bullying, racism, discrimination, etc.) and malpractices in different institutions (patient neglect, ineffective restructurings, cost-cutting practices that endanger the public, etc.) and failing to be heard. In the UK-based 'Campaign for Social Science', this argument formed the basis of a report called 'The Business of People: The significance of Social Science over the Next Decade' (2015, p. xi), whose authors claim:

> The challenges facing the UK—its prosperity and functioning as a place for trade, creativity, exchange, equity, and opportunity—will be met only if we deploy social science knowledge, skills and methods of inquiry ever more intensively. To thrive we must innovate. In innovation, we must marry progress in technology and the physical and life sciences with insights from studying behaviour, place, economy and society.

The report puts forward the view that many of today's problems and challenges can only be addressed by scientists acting across disciplinary boundaries and capable of influencing politicians and other power-holders through the force of their arguments, a view widely shared across social science. But if social science harbours such great ambitions, how come it has not solved the problem of its own irrelevance? Is there anything social scientists could do differently to make their work more meaningful to people outside academia? We believe there is, and as a first step towards this goal, we argue that social scientists have to become better at questioning the meaning of what they (we) do.

This, then, is the core argument of our book. The current proliferation of academic publications in social science, far from enhancing human knowledge, is creating a vacuum of meaning. We are not claiming that all publications are meaningless or nonsensical, but we do claim that a substantial part of them are, with only rare examples offering a rich empirical study or an insight that impresses the well-informed reader. Materials that scholars prepare as part of their academic apprenticeship which in the past would have been consigned to the filing cabinet of 'Juvenilia' are currently being published in ostensibly respectable journals; other publications, following the rigours of academic reviews and numerous revisions, are virtually emptied of any originality or substance. Academic publishing has turned into a game where careers are forged and departmental reputations are manufactured on the back of 'hits'. These are formulaic and hollow publications in journals themselves engaged in the game of impact factors which further enhances formulaic and meaningless publications. The game certainly makes sense to the players and the stakes are quite high but its consequences are in many ways negative. Meaningless papers do not merely fail to have any impact with the social challenges that urgently confront us, but they spread cynicism and fatalism among the participants and reinforce instrumentalism. They also clutter the sphere of knowledge with noise so that truly original and meaningful publications have less chance of being developed, noticed, discussed, and acted upon. They intensify disciplinary boundaries and enhance the existence of academic microtribes which carefully monitor access to publications, exercising a conservative effect on new ideas and new methods as well as on cross-tribe collaborations. The result is a sphere of largely meaningless and purposeless knowledge. We claim that the production of such knowledge is far from without cost. It prevents academics from dedicating more time and care to their students, it stops them from reading those works that have something original and meaningful to say, it raises the costs of higher education to students and taxpayers, and it even encourages meaningless competition and endless self-promotion among academics themselves.

According to many academics 'the spread of proxy metrics, the target culture, competition between institutions, the erosion of the autonomy of academic research and professional priorities and imported productivity mechanisms such as performance management regimes' lead to the proletarianization of contemporary academics. The author, a professor in geography, continues:

The encroachment of the managerial logic and mode of evaluation (proxy metrics) into all areas leads to the erosion of fundamental features that escape audit: professional integrity and collegiality. Instead, patterns of instrumental behaviour aimed at absorbing bureaucratic pressure proliferate, along with cynicism and even contempt towards management imperatives. (Brandist, *THE*, 5 May, 2016)

Other authors go so far to talk about academic zombies (e.g. Ryan, 2012), the living dead, claiming that strict regimes make people respond rather mindlessly to demands and stimuli rather than themselves being full agents and carriers of meaning. These are somewhat extreme views, and may be outbursts of frustrations rather than nuanced descriptions, and there are definitively many that experience things differently (Clarke et al., 2012) or only partly agree (Knights & Clarke, 2014; Kallio et al., 2016), but the harsh statements and efforts to wake up both over-adaptive academics and insensitive and technocratric policy-makers are worth noting.

We recognize that the causes of this situation are many and diverse. They include the rise of new technologies that make the composition, circulation, and dissemination of texts infinitely easier than they have ever been in the past; the increasing consumerism and credentialism that suffuses higher education; the practices of academic journals, publishers, research institutions, accrediting and ranking bodies, universities, and governments. We can also note the expansion of administration to such a level that the majority of UK universities now employ more administrators than teachers and researchers (Jump, 2015). A key cause is the vast expansion of higher education in recent decades, the resulting lowering of quality and the falling status of academics and institutions—something that intensifies competition for status and reputation within the academic circles. It also fuels a focus on quantitative indicators—number of publications in ranked journals and citations—as no one has an overview and qualitative judgement gets lost outside small micro-tribes of specialized researchers. Research, especially quantifiable outputs and publications in the right journals, has emerged as the key to enhanced individual and institutional status and reputations—hence, in a desperate attempt to improve their standing and prospects, academics, encouraged by their institutions as much as by their individual ambitions, are blindly producing volumes of research publications with very little concern for its social meaning or value.

Against this background, it would be naïve if we claimed that this little book by itself will enable social researchers to reclaim meaning for the work that they do and will reconnect social science with the pressing needs of our societies. We do, however, believe that the book opens certain possibilities and makes certain concrete proposals which will at least enhance the reader's ability, whether as editor, reviewer, academic, publisher, or citizen to raise the profile of meaningfulness as a key aim of academic research. In making these proposals, it should not be thought that we are exempting ourselves from responsibility for meaningless work. Far from it. As academics, we are very aware in our daily practices of the pressures to publish no matter what the substance of the publication is and we have, like most others—bar Stoner—to deal with these pressures, including internalized pressures to demonstrate for ourselves how smart and effective we are. We are confident, however, that many in social science share our concerns and that the proposals we put forward in the second part of this book will make a contribution to ongoing efforts to recover meaning and value for social science.

What we Mean by 'Meaning'

In recognizing some of our own failings, we acknowledge that the recovery of meaning presents us, as social scientists, with some special challenges. In our professional, just as in our personal lives, we all too often are engaged in activities that 'make sense' to us within a narrow framework. We invest a lot of time and effort reading the works of others, analysing, drawing distinctions, observing paradoxes and inconsistencies, distilling arguments and counterarguments, and absorbing large amounts of information. We also sometimes agonize in writing our own texts, we critique, we juxtapose, we infer, and we dismiss. We respond to criticisms and comments by other scholars and, undoubtedly, seek to enhance our own positions and reputations. In all these ways we are engaged, as Weick (1995) has rightly argued, in a constant process of sensemaking of our own and other people's actions and works. Yet, a fundamental premise of this book is that sensemaking is not the same as doing something meaningful. Many things make sense; for example, a lot of bureaucratic routines, even if they have little or no meaning. Much research output makes perfect sense in terms of career aspirations and institutional pressures, even if it produces little of lasting meaning or substance for ourselves or for others.

Critical scholars approaching the question of meaning start from the premise that meaning, especially the meaning of work, cannot be separated from prevailing power relations in society. In his early work on alienated labour, Marx (1844/1972) proposed that under capitalist conditions of production, a large part of human labour becomes alienated. The meaning of work becomes systematically distorted as a part of alienated consciousness that inevitably results from capitalist production. Alienated consciousness consistently misreads the meaning of commodities as well as the meaning of human actions, relations, and of work itself. Material and symbolic commodities and the labour that goes in producing them—they all make a lot of sense to the alienated being, even if their meaning is systematically distorted. Scholars, following Marx and other critical traditions, claim for themselves the special privilege of being able to see beyond the effects of alienation, to demystify taken-for-granted meanings, to denaturalize what appear as commonsensical or inevitable, and to probe into meanings that are systematically distorted or concealed. Psychoanalytic scholarship has amplified the view that meanings are systematically distorted by proposing that the conscious meanings of our beliefs, our actions, and our creations (e.g. Freud, 1930) frequently conceal deeper, unconscious meanings that, were they to reach consciousness, would result in anxiety, guilt, shame, and other unbearable emotions. A key element for many academics is the narcissism involved in doing and publishing research. The self is invested in the work and research publications function as reinforcers and stabilizers of a sense of self susceptible to the insecurities and vulnerabilities of a profession consistently exposed to assessment and a level of competition where failures greatly outscore successes for most people—as efforts to publish in highly-ranked journals and with prestigious publishing houses often lead to 90 per cent rejections. The bitterness and aggression most academics experience against journals, editors, and reviewers demonstrates a profound sense of unfairness associated with the narcissistic injuries of the academic, with grand contributions to humankind, facing the pettiness of a non-gratifying world. The recovery of meaning, therefore, is not a simple matter—it involves working against formidable social and psychological forces that seek to normalize comforting illusions and wish-fulfilling rationalizations.

Phenomenologists use the term 'meaning' in a more detached sense as 'reflected experience'. In a 'stream of consciousness', many things ('phenomena') pass us by without reflection or thought, like images captured in a security camera. These are, by definition, devoid of meaning. As Schutz puts it, 'the problem of meaning is a time problem' (Schutz, 1967, p. 12). Meaning must be created either before or after we become conscious of an experience or perform an action. The ego thus actively *constructs* meaning out of the stream of consciousness, but meaning itself cannot be constructed independently of the phenomena—it is a part of consciousness in which all phenomena register. Nor does each individual create meaning in a vacuum. *Social* meaning is constructed inter-subjectively through pre-phenomenal fusions of horizons that we build in social interaction (Schutz, 1967, pp. 133–4). In this latter sense, meaning may be studied as a detached phenomenon of its own, especially as it appears in signs, in a way that comes close to semiotics.

One of the central issues that has concerned phenomenologists has been the increasing difficulty that humans have in creating meaning in modern society. The decline of religion and politics as great unifying cultural forces leads to a proliferation and fragmentation of meaning systems. Technology, mass travel and tourism, and the mass media constantly undermine traditional value and belief systems. The same goes for consumerism—where post-affluence leads to material objects assuming restless, fleeting, and superficial meanings, and where the seductive powers of 'the brand' reign supreme. Constant contact with other cultures has made us keenly aware of the relativity of meaning systems—the heroes of one culture are the social outcasts of another, practices praised and honoured in one culture are severely condemned and punished in another. Also within a culture there are highly contested and fluctuating meanings. People are expected to act in line with norms for gender-appropriate behaviour while avoiding stereotyping themselves or others. Whistleblowers are admired at a distance, but seen as traitors to be condemned within the organization or occupation exposed. The relativity of meaning, argued Becker (1962), threatens humans with the death of meaning, a terrifying prospect of having nothing to live for or nothing firm to hold on to. In such a universe, Frankl writes, each individual is called upon to create his/her own individual meaning system, a formidable challenge. The quest for meaning becomes, for Frankl (Frankl, 1984 [1956], p. 121), the 'primary motivational force in man [sic]' against the terrifying threat of *meaninglessness*, when individuals 'are haunted by the experience of their inner emptiness, a void within themselves; they are caught in that situation which I have called the "existential vacuum"' (Frankl, 1984 [1956], p. 128). Similarly, for Arendt, 'meaningless' represents the 'devaluation of all values' (Arendt, 1958, p. 236).

In putting forward our own vision of meaningful research, we take from Marxism the idea that meaning systems are linked to power relations in society; we take from psychoanalysis a fundamental questioning on the innocence of meanings and the ease with which we may deceive ourselves; and we take from phenomenology the important insight that the quest for meaning strives for something of purpose and value, that is more than *comprehensible*. A piece of research can be based upon rigorous methods, it can make a clear 'contribution to the field', it can be published in a respectable journal and be cited—and yet it can be quite meaningless. It may fail in offering genuine understanding and insights, a genuine experience of wonder and surprise or in providing any guide for action. To understand the concept of meaningful research, we propose to draw two fundamental distinctions: first, the distinction between meaningful work and meaningful product and, second, meaningful to the ego versus meaningful to a specific group or to wider society.

A significant part of research activity by an individual or a group may be meaningful without generating anything of wider meaning or value. Many meaningful activities lead to meaningless products. This is especially true when an activity has the quality of 'practice'—students do a lot of sketches as a means to attaining mastery but most of these sketches have little meaning for the wider society beyond enabling an individual to 'discover his/her voice' or to develop his/her skill. In this way, many confused, formulaic, unoriginal, and mundane texts can be the product of meaningful activity on the part of their authors, part of their training to become better researchers, without achieving any higher purpose or meaning. Moreover, many efforts by seasoned researchers may not lead to anything of higher purpose or meaning. This is in the nature of research itself—the quest for knowledge all too frequently leads to dead ends, trivial discoveries, mundane realizations, or simply confirmations of what is already widely known and accepted. The quest may have been meaningful—guided by the best of intentions—but the end product has been of little significance. As Cavafy concludes in his poem 'Ithaca', the meaning of many journeys lies in the journey itself rather than the discovery once we reach our destination. It takes courage and self-awareness to be able to acknowledge that such quests, meaningful in themselves, have not generated anything of wider meaning and purpose.

The second distinction we draw is between three spheres of meaningfulness:

Meaningful to the ego. Just as the activity of research itself, a piece of research—an article, a monograph, a seminar paper including the process that yields these products—can be meaningful to the researchers individually in the sense that they feel their study makes their lives worth living. Curiosity, hedonism, challenge, and even simple careerism can act as powerful—and positive—individual motivators. (These will be examined in detail in Chapter 4.) Researchers may also have the sense of contributing something to other people or to some higher principle. This, however, can all too easily be shown to be the product of wishfull thinking or self-deception.

Meaningful to a specific group. A way of validating if one's research contributes to other people is to see whether it is meaningful to a particular group. This group can be an employer, a union, a client, but most frequently it is a research microtribe with which the researcher identifies. Presenting papers at gatherings of a microtribe, writing and reviewing for its journals, and so on, has a ceremonial quality, sometimes deeply meaningful to the participants. The meaning of such work is quite *esoteric*, limited to those who have been initiated into a particular way of thinking, jargon-mastery, and acting, which makes little sense or has no significance to outsiders. Most academic writings in journals have the character of addressing themselves only to members of particular microtribes, caring little about reaching wider audiences, even people generally interested in the subject matter.

Meaningful to the wider society, i.e. research that reaches out beyond the interests of specific groups. Here the idea is to go beyond a specific, narrow target group of academic or professional specialists and generate knowledge of value to society as a whole. Parts of the educated or in other ways interested public are then addressed and reached. This does not imply popularization, but the work with ideas, empirical material and texts, and publication formats that reaches beyond the narrow concerns of specialists.

Research that is meaningful to the wider society does not have to be comprehensible to all. Studies in natural science and medicine can be meaningful despite the fact that most people cannot understand them. As mentioned, they have, at least sometimes, an instrumental value evident in the effects of their applications: the new treatment for a disorder, the environmentally friendlier engine, or the new methods for growing plants in depleted soil. Some abstract or fundamental research in theoretical physics or mathematics may not have immediate applications but can still claim to be meaningful to wider society as part of a universal desire for understanding and knowledge.

Research in social science is *potentially* meaningful to wider society if it addresses the political, economic, or existential realities that face it and affect the lives of the public. Whether or not this potential is realized depends on whether the study is available for public scrutiny, which, in turn, requires for it to be communicated in a widely comprehensible way. Many studies, as we noted earlier, remain hidden in journals to which most people do not have access. They are also hidden by a format and by linguistic fetters that make their relevance hard to evaluate, even for those who do have access. Our own home discipline(s), work and organization studies, for example, is an area that addresses the concerns of most people—not only managers, but politicians, unions, employees, clients, and other stakeholders, all of whom may have a say on whether it is meaningful or useful to them. If organizational research is only communicated internally and circulated within a narrow academic microtribe, most legitimate stakeholders may wonder what its purpose or meaning may be. We do not claim that *all* research has to address broader and non-specialist groups. There certainly are areas of abstract or inward-looking theorizing, methodology, and reflexivity that can be predominantly of interest to academics. This can be important work that indirectly proves valuable to broader audiences by inspiring work more relevant to 'end-users' of knowledge outside academia. Some such work is necessary (and this book belongs in part to this category) but should not dominate at the expense of research with the ambition to have something to say to broader audiences.

When juxtaposing the spheres of meaningfulness and studying their overlaps as in Figure 1.1, we see different types of meaningfulness (and meaninglessness) that tend to be confused in the debates on academic writing. Some of it (*a* in Figure 1.1) is characterized by a complete lack of meaning, not necessarily in the sense that it is total nonsense as in the Sokal and the other examples mentioned earlier, but more often in the sense that it is of no value to anyone, not even to the individual pursuing the research. A typical example that most academics will encounter is the disillusioned PhD student who just wants to 'get done with the thesis'. Both the activity and the product of research become depleted of almost all meaning, beyond the narrowest

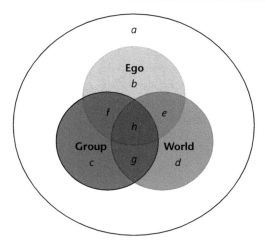

Figure 1.1. Overlapping spheres of meaningfulness

instrumental value of the award of a PhD. This may be of some use to the researcher (who can claim some measure of success for his/her effort and a certificate to demonstrate it) and the institution (which is pleased to rid itself of such a PhD student and improve output statistics). Yet, there is no real value in such situations—only alienated labour resulting in a suffocating feeling of meaninglessness to all involved. We believe that this is far from rare.

Sometimes research can be deeply meaningful to an individual but to no one else (*b*), as in the case of bookworms who may lose themselves in their reading, or those who write with no concern whether their work will be read or appreciated by anyone else. On other occasions, as in the case of alienated research assistants who primarily work to earn a living, the product of their labour (e.g. interview transcripts, experiment results, quantitative data) may only be meaningful to the group that has commissioned the work (*c*), which does not preclude it from being meaningful to the wider society (*g*).

A more frequent overlap is research that is meaningful to an individual researcher and his/her group, but that leaves anyone outside the group bewildered or simply unaware of it (*f*). Some of this work may entail an indirect contribution to wider society, one that is yet to be discovered—which would lead straight to the bull's-eye (*h*)—but, much more likely, along with the entire research field to which it belongs, it remains obscure, incomprehensible, and meaningless to wider society.

Meaningful research generally has some value and interest for all three 'interest spheres', including a part of the world outside the academic subgroup of the researcher. Meaning then occupies the position *h* in the figure above. As we said earlier, some research that scores high on intra-scientific meaningfulness (*f*) may compensate for lack of wider relevance or meaningfulness outside the intra-academic subgroup. If, however, only an individual researcher can vouch for the meaning of this work, then its social value is seriously called into question.

It is important not to be too categorical here. These issues are far from simple, and we try to encourage serious reflection and critical dialogue rather than crude tick-off exercises or counting readers/recipients of research. Research firmly in sphere (*f*) or even (*b*) (e.g. the work of a rare solitary genius) may occasionally diffuse to (*h*) and assume significance for wider society. Besides, not all research in (*h*) is necessarily beneficial to all of society. Particular research ideas and findings may be seductive, may match the zeitgeist, may correspond to their owners' wishful thinking or prejudices, or serve sectional interests of particular stakeholders. Rothstein (2015) notes that politicians may find political science studies of particular interest if they can be used to support their own interests vis-à-vis those of others:

> Political science could be relevant for giving advice on how to win election campaigns, how politicians should best act so as to get enough support for their policies in legislative assemblies, when and if state leaders should go to war or how they should act in international negotiations for best furthering the interests of their countries, to name a few.

Meaningfulness is not the same as interest, popularity, or fashion. Careful critical scrutiny of research contributions is always vital, and the question of meaningful knowledge contribution must meet intra-academic criteria as well as having something important to say to some people. If the latter group is small, the knowledge contribution needs to be significant. If you can only talk to a few people, it seems vital that you have a lot to say to them, for your research to be fairly judged to be meaningful.

It should be emphasized that research that is meaningful to others is not necessarily a straightforward, simple, or even good thing. A management group, government, profession, or union may welcome knowledge that technically or ideologically supports its interests, possibly at the expense of others whose interests are equally or even more legitimate. Also the public may be attracted to knowledge that promises a bright future or confirms public prejudice, for example, about a knowledge society or the expansion of the 'creative class'. Having something meaningful to say, as we advocate in this book, requires that we move beyond sectional interests, fashionable clichés, and faddish pseudo-theories and ask seriously how our research serves some common good (Spicer et al., 2009).

In Conclusion

This book's purpose is to describe the current problem of meaninglessness that afflicts much social science research, to identify the reasons for it, and to indicate some possible ways of recovering meaning in the work we do as researchers. Such an aim would be futile if we were alone in our concern. We believe, however, that we are part of a rising climate of opinion among social scientists disturbed by the huge amounts of esoteric or meaningless research and texts requiring extensive labour that are currently being produced, but are virtually irrelevant. We are also part of a world facing innumerable and daunting challenges: political, environmental, economic, ethical; while many social scientists pursue their Quixotic agendas oblivious to the suffering, conflict, social dislocation, alienation, oppression, and—in particular—stupidity that surrounds them.

Some of our recommendations are highly specific and even parochial. Others are more far-reaching. They include institutional reforms that will reduce the emphasis on research and relatedly the pressure to publish; systematic efforts to upgrade the status of teaching and pedagogy; more opportunities for 'everyone' in academia to engage in scholarship and scholarly dialogue (seminars, reading, less focus on researchers writing, reviewing, editing, and publishing papers); a radical reconfiguration of career options; a downplaying of instrumental rewards coupled to publications; and a reinvigoration of the social relevance of academic research. We will propose new ideals for social research: new ideas for managing higher education institutions; different forms of publication and dissemination of scholarly work; new criteria of relevance and impact. We will also propose new assessments and rankings of academic institutions based not solely or predominantly on quantity and presumed prestige of research publications, but on a more limited number of socially, intellectually, and scientifically significant contributions. In all these ways, *we therefore call for a radical move from research for the sake of publishing to research that has something meaningful to say*. We recognize that a return to meaningful research and scholarship will necessitate deep-seated changes in the functioning of institutions and policies, as well as the ways in which academics construct their professional identities. Such a return, however, would place the formidable intellectual, cultural, and educational resources of social science to the service of the societies that support it.

Although many are responsible for this sad state of affairs and the steady decline of social science, we feel that much blame lies with researchers like ourselves, in particular senior ones. It is popular to attribute all evils to policies, governments, university management, competition, rankings, and so forth. But we believe that academics, who spend significant amounts of time and resources on their research, carry a substantial responsibility for its value, relevance, and meaning. We also believe that it is reasonable that research-active scholars should be expected, every few years, to present four good publications reflecting the quality of their work. Some performance pressure and measurement is not necessarily bad. As individuals and members of a collective, we in the social sciences can be expected to offer a great deal more to society than we have been able to deliver in recent decades. Much can be done within the academic communities and by individual academics undertaking more ambitious, creative, and socially relevant research, countering the embarrassing trend that more and more is published that seems to have less and less to say.

Increased frustrations and critiques indicate that the current system is not sustainable over the long term. The cost of higher education, born mainly by taxpayers, students, and their parents is becoming prohibitive, while at the same time the quality of the service they receive is downgraded. Increasing numbers of academics, especially in social science, are in some countries afflicted by job insecurity, declining income and status, and growing work pressures that are adversely affecting their health and ability to do creative work (See *The Times Higher Education Good Workplace Survey* for an increasingly bleak picture of rising discontent and despair among academics). Technological forces enable the rapid dissemination of huge numbers of works of dubious meaning and value, making the need for meaningful social research with something of value to say to wider society more pressing. For all of these reasons, it is our firm belief that the arguments put forward in this book should become part of a growing discussion in support of recovering meaning for social research.

2

From Science as a Vocation to Science as a Game: and the Resulting Loss of Meaning

The loss of meaning currently afflicting social science is not only the result of developments in higher education, but must be seen as part of the wider crisis of meaning in western societies, coinciding with the advent of modernity, urban living, scientific knowledge, and bureaucratic organizations (including universities). In *The Birth and Death of Meaning* (1962), Ernest Becker argued that the rise of science had substantially shaken some of humanity's most cherished beliefs. For millennia, these beliefs had filled people's lives with uncontested meaning. As Freud had observed earlier, the Copernican revolution destroyed the belief that the earth is the centre of the universe just as the Darwinian revolution shook the conviction that 'man' was God's privileged and much loved creation. As a cultural anthropologist, Becker argued that the increased contact between cultures since the early twentieth century brought about a realization that meaning and value systems are relative. What is valued by one culture is disparaged by another; what is praised in one culture is censured in another. There are no meanings in history apart from those invested in it by historical human actors. There are no fixed points in ethics, politics, aesthetics, or anything else on which meaning may reliably be fastened. Instead, every culture and every individual, argued Becker, is faced with the colossal task of creating and sustaining meaning, without which humans are abandoned to terrifying existential anxieties and death. However, humanity knows these meanings to be ephemeral and provisional.

Creating and maintaining such meanings requires what Becker called the invention of 'hero systems', clusters of beliefs and values against which every person can construct him/herself as a subject and an object of self-esteem and value. Writing some thirty years before the mushrooming of interest in identity, Becker was essentially addressing the same question. Identity, the place of each individual in the world, is not a simple matter but one that requires constant work, as people seek to infuse their experience with meaning and turn themselves into worthy characters in their life stories. A central feature of contemporary heroism for Becker is 'the power to support contradictions, no matter how glaring or hopeless they may seem' (p. 196). Late modernity with the spasmodic rise and fall of postmodernism, its prolonged undermining of universal humanist ethics and values, the rise of consumerism, the growth of multiculturalism, and the explosion of information technologies has brought about further erosions of taken-for-granted meaning systems and values. Consumer culture with its incessant noise as brands struggle to be heard and noticed, ends up by creating black holes into which meaning disappears. Yesterday's global 'icon' turns into today's discarded junk; today's bright celebrity liable to become tomorrow's forgotten has-been. Signifiers, meanings, identities, along with everything else, come and go at the blink of an eyelid.

What is the role of science, including social science, in all this? In his celebrated lecture 'Science as a vocation', Max Weber (1946) cast scientific knowledge as the major force behind what he called 'the disenchantment of the world', a force which depletes every experience, including death, from meaning. 'Who, aside from certain big children who are indeed found in the natural sciences', he asks, 'still believes that the findings of astronomy, biology, physics, or chemistry could teach us anything about the *meaning* of the world? If there is any such "meaning", along what road could one come upon its tracks? If these natural sciences lead to anything in this way, they are apt to make the belief that there is such a thing as the "meaning" of the universe die out at its very roots.' Weber's conclusion is stark. Siding with Tolstoy, he concludes that 'Science is meaningless because it gives no answer to our question, the only question important for us: "What shall we do and how shall we live?"' Weber is particularly scathing about the ability of social and political sciences, 'the disciplines close to me', arguing that while capable of analysing different phenomena they are unable to establish the ultimate value of ideals like democracy, of institutions like religion, or even the value of knowledge itself.

As is alluded to by the expression 'big children' above, Weber was aware that scientists themselves invest their activities with meaning, and sometimes big meanings: progress, the emancipation of humanity from need, and so forth. Hence 'science as a vocation' involves a quasi-religious calling, a passionate devotion, a steely discipline, a preparedness to make sacrifices, a faith in scientific method and a belief in progress, all of which distinguish the scientist from the dilettante. Like priests, scientists pursue their vocation in a dead-serious manner, believing that what they do is deeply meaningful. Yet, unlike priests, scientists have not been granted the gift of creating meaning. Weber explicitly contrasts scientists to prophets, artists, and leaders who address questions of meaning and value and firmly concludes that the best the scientist can offer is clarity as to the means for achieving specific ends: *'If* you take such and such a stand, then, according to scientific experience, you have to use such and such a *means* in order to carry out your conviction practically' (emphasis in the original). Unlike religion and politics, science is unable to provide meanings for the sufferings of the world or to allay humanity's deep-seated anxieties about matters of life and death.

A thinker with a more equivocal appreciation of the role of science was Freud, even though his ultimate concern was not with meaning but rather with pleasure and happiness (1930). In this regard, he acknowledged that scientific discoveries have freed humans from many of the threats and dangers of nature, have opened up many new avenues for pleasure and fulfilment, not least by enabling us to enjoy the fruits of culture, art, and literature. All the same, Freud was no uncritical enthusiast of science and its technological fruits, noting repeatedly how these achievements, far from allaying people's deep anxieties, actually create anxieties of their own. To be sure, the know-ledge that an antibiotic may cure a routine infection or that a phone will put us in touch with our loved ones is reassuring. Playing a computer game can be exhilarating. Having the options of a huge range of food, clothes, reading materials, entertainment, self-enhancement, and leisure to choose from is seductive. Yet Freud argued that science has failed to make humans substan-tially happier or freer, since every new scientific discovery and every new technological advance creates new dependencies, risks, and fears.

What, however, Freud saw as the immense value of scientific knowledge, is its ability to dispel illusions (including religious ones), superstitions, and falsehoods which promise to deliver happiness and end up by deepening human discontents. He also credited it with the pleasure of discovery; the quest for an understanding of how the world, both inner and outer, functions through critical inquiry. Defending his 'God Logos' drew from Freud some of his most passionate writings, arguing that the meanings of phenomena revealed by science may lack the cosmic certainty and sweep of religious or political ideologies, but are capable of constant correction and improvement. What differentiates Freud's more optimistic outlook from Weber's is his belief that science cannot be detached from a humanistic ethos of reducing human suffering in all its forms, and supporting an agenda of social justice, freedom, and happiness.[1]

---

[1] Interestingly, Weber differentiated between what he called the 'scientist' and the 'intellectual'. Intellectuals include, in Weber's vocabulary, religious persons who, like Freud, seek not only to clarify but to give solutions to social problems relating to meaning. This can also be an egoistic endeavour of the intellectual: 'The intellectual seeks in various ways, the casuistry of which extends into infinity, to endow his life with a pervasive meaning, and thus to find unity with himself, with his fellow men, and with the cosmos. It is the intellectual who conceives of the "world" as a problem of meaning' (Weber, 1978 [1922], p. 506). For Weber, intellectuals thus have wider, more personal but also less disciplined ways of attaining meaning.

From Science as Vocation to Science as a Game

Where Freud and Weber were in agreement was in their approach to the pursuit of scientific truth in quasi-religious tones of vocation and the 'God Logos'. They certainly were elitist enough to assume that the spirit of scientific inquiry is available only to a limited number of people called to the profession, that doing scientific research is a serious matter, and that there is a world of difference between the genuine scientist and the amateur or dilettante. However, this is hardly applicable, at least in social science today, when research and publishing have assumed the character of a 'game'. This is now taken for granted in most casual conversations among researchers, it is reinforced by 'Meet the editors' sessions that feature in every major conference, and is constantly debated in academic publications (Butler & Spoelstra, 2012; Courpasson, Arellano-Gault, Brown, & Lounsbury, 2008; Grey, 2010). Learning to play the publishing game has rapidly become part of the core curriculum of most PhD training courses and is the topic of innumerable invitations to speak received by editors of major journals. Playing the publishing game effectively is now essential for an academic career, and a skill without which no amount of devotion and scholarship can find recognition. In sharp opposition to the quasi-religious concepts of Weber and Freud, the prevailing view of the academic researcher now is more akin to a gamesman, involved in all kinds of games in order to achieve the much longed for 'hits' in top journals.

The consequences of the academic publishing game are far-reaching. Journals, from low-ranked to prestigious ones, emerge not so much as spaces for sharing and testing scholarship but as career machines determining promotions and tenures, and as arenas for a fierce competition among academics with relatively few winners and many losers. There are glittering, if short-lived prizes to be won by simply having one's name in a starred publication. There are victories and defeats, and even consolation prizes in eventually having one's work accepted in a less prestigious outlet.

Competition among academics is neither new nor necessarily harmful. It is generally both unavoidable and potentially productive. Competition can promote hard work, innovation, and excellence. Ideally it allows for the screening out of less good contributions. It has long been part of the ethos of scientific research as Weber himself recognizes in 'Science as a vocation'. Envy for the success of others and a strong narcissistic belief in the merit of one's own work, no matter how little recognition it may receive, have long been features of scientific inquiry. This is evidenced in the long-standing and fierce disputes over the claims to priority of specific discoveries, such as calculus, evolution, and the HIV virus. This is sometimes positive; critical debate is vital within science as there are few absolute truths. Current competition among researchers, however, has some distinct and potentially detrimental qualities.

The winners and losers of this competition lack the enduring qualities that earned respect and status for scholars in the past. Increasingly, researchers are judged by the prestige of their latest publication or number of publications rather than by their cumulative contributions to scholarship, or for having made a substantive contribution that stands out and makes a real difference. Seldom does a paper really stand out—most authors play it safe and produce formulaic and largely meaningless papers, and even those who set their sights at more ambitious goals often find it difficult to say something significant that has not been said before. Very few contributions become the objects of great interest and careful assessment and debates outside microtribes—and also within these, for that matter. Most and more contributions are 'yawn-papers'. Very few lead to the response 'this is interesting' that calls for something unexpected and counterintuitive, deviating from the well-hammered-in frameworks and vocabularies most researchers are eager to reproduce (Davis, 1971).

Given the decrease in clear, original, and outstanding qualities of papers, the publication form becomes more central. Competition centres less around good ideas and valuable contributions and more around how many articles journals researchers have published. Once again, this is not wrong—it is probably often an outcome of diligent and good work if people are productive and manage to publish in highly-ranked journals. But this has taken the upper hand and is often not a guarantee for socially valuable knowledge contributions.

Ephemeral success is a feature of journal publishing in social science which is often sensitive to academic fashions, where different theories and approaches compete for ascendancy and frequently rise and decline with the rapidity of fashion brands. There are two, almost opposite, risks here. One is working solely within a research microtribe or box, that is, a narrow subfield and addressing others in the small community of like-minded researchers (Alvesson & Sandberg, 2014). Young researchers who tie their future to the success of a single brand or theory may be highly successful as they know the assumptions, expectations, and rules of the microtribe and can manoeuvre effectively. They can also exploit their knowledge and skills and mass produce their papers, without necessarily developing any familiarity with other fields. But they are also liable to see their careers decline with the fortunes of their brand, whether this is a particular perspective or theory, an individual thinker, a methodology, a philosophy, or even a particular craft in the execution of their work. Researchers who invested heavily into postmodernism in the 1990s had their moment in the sun but much of the published work from those days is now viewed as esoteric and obsolete.

The second problem is almost the opposite. The ability to play on several different tables or fields without becoming too closely attached to any single one has become the trademark of the fast-moving, flexible, and effective player, the one who can readily switch from one area to another as academic fashions dictate. For example, the expert in statistical techniques can use number-crunching skills to produce results without any deeper knowledge or original thinking about a subject matter. A specific problem here is the expanded use of big data and the easiness of finding something significant that may give the impression of a credible 'contribution'. As a professor in economics has observed:

> With econometric techniques being more and more sophisticated, I find the eternal hunt for causality and the establishment of some significant correlation that has gone through hundreds of robustness tests sometimes hilarious in light of the fact that research gets published with an overall R^2 of less than 0.05, and the individual coefficient of interest explaining only marginal differences in the dependent variable. Some fields are particularly vulnerable, health economics (which sounds socially relevant) is one of them. Also the rapidly growing avail- ability of big data sets combining 100,000 of observations makes it easy to find the oh-so-important correlation and then to construct by means of reverse engineer- ing a fitting story line.   (Personal communication)

A resulting problem is that many researchers fail to master any particular area of scholarship or to think deeper about social phenomena. Instead, there is a premium to be content to vacuum-clean ever narrower areas of literature controlled by their microtribe or become a virtuoso in a specific method or technique. But the 'boxed-in' contributor to a subfield and the opportunistic and shallow fashion-follower (area hopper) are two common, possibly increasingly so, academic characters that both are unlikely to make meaningful contributions.

The motives of the publishing game are quite different from those of researchers who approached science as a vocation. Survival and eventual rise up the slippery pole, including rapid (over-)promotion, financial benefits, invitations, and other instrumental rewards replace the passion for discovery and the intrinsic quest for knowledge. Discovery without outputs in presti- gious outlets becomes meaningless; delight in discovery for its own sake becomes an exception. 'How can I get published' rather than 'how can I do good research' becomes the burning question. Survival and eventual success in the publishing game dictates a close understanding of its strange and imprecise formulas, its conventions and its peculiarities. Knowing that X has published a paper in journal Y on topic Z becomes infinitely more important than engaging with X's arguments, critically scrutinizing them, and having a meaningful dialogue with them, although if one is about to meet X in a conference and X is a celebrated researcher of interest for 'networking', it may be good to be able to offer some positive remarks about the content.

The competition among researchers to capture the limelight and make their voices heard against a profusion of noise is paralleled by the competition among journals in the game for impact factors and citations. The advent of electronic searches and the meticulous recording of the ballooning store of references and citations has led to the growth of bibliometrics. This is a mixed blessing. Positively it can be a counterforce to arbitrary opinions and nepotism as it brings in some indications of the interest and respect from the academic community as a whole to the works of specific academics. There is a tendency that original and important work is being picked up and cited. Few citations can indicate that not even the academic subtribe pay any notice. This may offer important feedback. More negatively, it can result in a fetishism of citations, where the worth of a piece of academic research is rigidly tied to the standing of the journal where it is published and the number of times it is cited. A number of ranking agencies (often with no academic expertise) have entered the field of evaluating the merits of academic outlets, further tightening the criteria by which research outputs are evaluated. It is in the nature of this competition to favour short and sharp measurements that can be updated every year, where the reputations and standings of different players in their leagues are constantly monitored. Minuscule rises and falls in individual players' positions in the rankings assume extraordinary significance, entirely unrelated to the quality of the work they produce. Short-termism and opportunism end up reigning supreme.

One outcome of the prevailing short-term mentality in social science has been the decline of monographs and books and the elevation of the 'research paper' to the universal currency of research merit. Many publishers have now ceased publishing monographs in social science altogether, focussing instead on the impact factors of their journals and the popularity of their textbooks. Others appear to accept almost anything for publishing, as they make money out of selling a limited number of books at high prices to libraries. Quality control is minimal. Where social scientists in the past may have written one or two books in a decade, following a review process arranged by the publisher, today's researchers are expected to publish on a continuous basis a steady stream of articles. The net result of all this has been an increasing conservatism in what is being published in top-ranked journals, with rigid standards for format and style (Alvesson & Gabriel, 2013), a tendency also present in journals lower down the rankings, which, however, may also publish rather wild or idiosyncratic papers of questionable merit and interest which remain generally unread and uncited. The only genre that might compete with journal articles in the game of science is that of research proposals written in order to be able to write articles. For reasons already stated, academics are extremely nervous about contributing to this genre. According to Herbert et al. (2013), 97 per cent of Australian researchers applying to the NHMRC (National Health and Medical Research Council) felt their proposals always took top priority over other work. In another study (Herbert, Barnett, &

Graves, 2013), they found that a single round of applying to the NHMRC represented an average of thirty-eight working days, representing in total 550 working years of researchers' time, which translates into an annual cost of AU $66 million. Since success rates are at best around 20 per cent, this represents a great waste both to researchers and to society at large.

Journal Publishing and its Discontents

The anonymous peer review is the cornerstone of the academic publishing game. Anonymity is indeed important in ensuring the quality of academic publications and reducing favouritism and discrimination. All the same, anonymous reviews create problems of their own, of which two have attracted attention: the demand for rigour; and the demand for novelty in a particular, rather limited sense. Of course, these demands are not always rigidly enforced; individual reviewers may choose to celebrate other aspects than rigour and incremental novelty. But there is a strong tendency that 'experts' in a subfield ask for close compliance with the norms of their subfield (or research box, as Alvesson & Sandberg 2014 call it.) Both demands have been widely debated, not least by journal editors who are now constantly grumbling on how difficult it is to receive meaningful papers to be published in their journals (Barley, 2016; Bedeian, 2003; Courpasson et al., 2008; Davis, 2015; Greenwood, 2016; Starbuck, 2003; Wellington & Nixon, 2005).

The demand for rigour—or rather a particular version of rigour—is one that accounts for the continuing preponderance of papers based on quantitative methodologies, no matter how trivial their conclusions. In an apocryphal story told by his students at Stanford (Barley, 2016, p. 4), organization studies and political science scholar James March once set an examination with a single mischievous question 'Name one paper that has made a theoretical contribution to organizational theory that also included a regression equation.' The story makes a point now widely acknowledged—most quantitative papers sacrifice meaning for rigour and rigour can best be purchased with sophisticated but routine statistics. Specialization reigns supreme as contributions focus on tiny 'gaps' in the literature. But the same sacrifice of meaning for rigour is now equally common in papers based on qualitative research. These dedicate lengthy sections on research methodology and the coding of text which has now assumed the standing of regression equations in quantitative papers. The increasing preoccupation with minutiae of methodology in pursuit of supposed rigour has led to increasingly formulaic papers seeking to fill ever narrower gaps in the literature. It may be thought that the demand for novelty would have the opposite effect—increasing originality.

Far from it. Novelty has come to be associated with infinitesimal contributions in ever narrower areas of research with relatively little concern for the meaning of these contributions or their ramifications.

Emphasis on rigour, incremental/limited novelty, and the resulting specialization have also led to another important development: increasing numbers of papers in social science are currently multi-authored. Disregarding the widespread practice of including in the list of authors the names of people who have made marginal or negligible contributions to the finished product, collaboration by several authors is meant to ensure that every potential objection raised by reviewers can be addressed. Different authors can then bring different areas of expertise to bear, plus their theories, methodologies, and even familiarity with the game as enacted by different journals, their editors, and reviewers. As with competition among researchers, there is nothing intrinsically wrong with multiple authorship—academic collaborations can generate cross-fertilizations and synergies of ideas, theories, and techniques which are capable of enhancing the quality of the research. Indeed, some of the classics in every field of social science are the product of collaborations between two or, very rarely, three authors. Unfortunately, however, this is rarely the case with many articles in social science today, when different parts of the article are parcelled off to different contributors, specialists in specific and narrow areas and often nobody in overall control of the paper. The result is writing by committee, a dilution of authorship, as few papers express the coherent voice and arguments of a particular scholar, emerging instead as collages of different, often incongruous, voices. Finding the right partners with whom to co-author a paper emerges as a crucial skill in the academic publishing game. Contributing to many multi-authored pieces can facilitate careers at the expense of a scholar's autonomy, originality, and distinct voice. (We are of course aware that this book is co-authored but leave it to the reader to assess the quality of the text in the light of our general complaints.)

The dilution of authorship is further exacerbated by the now common practice of submitting papers to endless revisions, following numerous exchanges with reviewers, each with their own interests and agendas. Even single-authored papers these days emerge after numerous reviews as over-blown and sanitized composites of arguments, tangents, digressions, detours, accretions, and other redundancies, resulting from the requests of different reviewers and editors, which are a far cry from what their author intended to express. Occasionally, this may enhance quality—better grounding in literature, more thought through and convincing arguments, and so on—but more often the demands for adaptation and compliance radically constrain autonomy and the author's voice. In this way, we may be witnessing the death of the author albeit not for the reasons envisaged by Barthes (1967/1977). Academics these days may fetishize the order in which their names feature in authors' lists, but in truth many articles are products of endless cutting and pasting, paraphrases, imitations, and parodies of other texts, a process hugely facilitated by electronic publication which lacks precisely the sense of a strong authorial voice driving an argument.

One inevitable consequence of the increasing gamesmanship of academic publishing is the erosion of the link between research and teaching, once the cornerstone of the Humboldtian university. Most of the papers published in social science journals seldom feed through into classroom teaching, and when they do, students often find the style and content off-putting, sometimes justifiably so. Academics only rarely find themselves being able to match teaching with the subjects that they are researching, relying on the standardized delivery methods of textbooks and accompanying materials to instruct the students. For some, especially the highly successful researchers, teaching becomes an annoying obligation, interfering with their writing time—notice, writing time, since reading time itself is seen as a nuisance and pushed to the margins of scholarship, reduced to cursory glances of abstracts and long lists of article titles, references, and authors churned up by databases. The greater the specialization required at the highest levels of the publishing game, the lesser the ability to maintain an overview of a wide field necessary to instruct students and develop their abilities. It is sometimes shocking to discover glaring gaps and holes in the knowledge of individuals with prestigious publication records. Equally shocking can be the reliance on secondary sources, including Wikipedia, by eminent scholars who occasionally are found out through careless plagiarism or replication of blatant errors.

All in all then, the transformation of scientific research from a vocation to a publishing game has had several adverse effects on the meaning and value of scientific knowledge, whether we take Freud's humanist view or Weber's more detached one. The assumptions that research should be of benefit to humanity or should serve a moral social agenda quickly evaporate in the heat of instrumentalist exigencies of academic careers, reviewers' and editors' requests, and the precariousness of academic status and position. Becoming noticed, even for a short while by a tiny group of individuals who may publish or cite your work, becomes paramount. Making your voice heard in the midst of the cacophony of publications becomes infinitely more significant than the content, quality, or purpose of the voice.

The Meaning of the Game

For players involved in any game, the meaning of the game is self-evident. Whether playing chess, baseball, or an electronic game known to few enthusiasts around the world, the participants' interest lies in playing the game, playing it well, enhancing their careers, and reaping the rewards of success. For audiences engrossed in a game, the question of meaning does not arise. What matters is who wins, who loses, who is rising, who is falling, and what profit can be made by taking stakes in the outcome of particular encounters. A game may be of no wider social significance, yet the willingness of people to play or watch the game offers ample justification for the game. The argument applies equally to the publishing game—in spite of the loss of wider social meaning, the game is profoundly important. The standing of individuals and institutions like universities and their different departments, journals and their positions in the rankings, and even students who select particular institutions in which to pursue their studies, all crucially depend on the outcomes of the game, no matter how irrelevant the game may be to the needs of society or how little benefit it generates for anyone outside its parameters. Arguably, even if the game is costly, involving a huge waste of time, money, and other resources, it persists as an institution enabling people to make sense of their everyday experiences. The logic of the game is to disregard everything that does not pertain to winning.

There are, however, some important differences between academic and most other forms of gaming. The latter have an intrinsic value and a sort of meaning. We play or watch a game because we like it; it gives us pleasure, the way that a piece of art can. Publishing as a game, on the other hand, derives its value mainly from the extent to which the end result is satisfying. It is purely instrumental; you play the game to win, otherwise, it is hardly worth it. And you sacrifice quite a lot in order to maximize the output. For many academics publishing is a pain-game rather than a pleasure-game. Given the endless complaints about journals, editors, and reviewers that we hear—often seen as preventing original and creative research—the painfulness and instrumental aspects seem to be increasingly salient.

The academic game, as we have noted earlier, is undoubtedly a hugely costly one, both for individuals and for societies, including taxpayers and students who, through their taxes and fees, finance the game. Large amounts of academic time that could be devoted to scholarship, teaching, and caring for students is spent on activities resulting in astronomical numbers of words being published, words that mostly go unread and whose main purpose is establishing the standing of individuals and institutions in the rankings. Everyone involved in the game may recognize that the game serves no superior purpose, but its logic is stifling. It may have no meaning and be painful but everything about it makes sense—the successes, the failure, even the (perceived) injustices and disappointments.

One of the factors that has undoubtedly contributed to the increasing meaninglessness of academic research has been a generalized loss of faith in the ability of science to address the major issues confronting societies today:

problems in schools, social work and health care, inequality, greed and corruption in public life, war, violence and mass dislocation of people in international affairs, environmental erosion, the threat of mass epidemics and climate change at the planetary level, and depression, anxiety, and psychological suffering at the individual level. Social science, in particular, has suffered from a questioning of humanistic ethics and an increasing conviction that behind noble pronouncements on the welfare of 'man' lie the interests of particular nations, classes, and groups. Education and learning themselves, far from being viewed as universal values in their own right, have come to be increasingly seen as instruments for gaining competitive advantage at the individual, group, or national levels. In some countries this is done through turning higher education, in particular business and management education, into an export business, where large numbers of overseas students are paying high fees for often questionable learning while counting on the exam for getting access to better jobs (Pfeffer & Fong, 2004). Knowledge is no longer assumed to be a universal resource enhancing the human spirit and promoting freedom from ignorance and servitude; instead, it is viewed as a resource to be managed and exploited for the advantage of particular groups. To the extent that it is acclaimed for its 'impact', it is acclaimed for its ability to open up new markets, new consumerist attractions, and new wealth-creating opportunities for business—enhancing the benefits of the few with little regard for the well-being of the many. This has resulted in a backlash, and some areas have become suspicious and critical of knowledge that is produced at the behest of particular groups, a tendency that risks throwing out the baby of socially useful and relevant knowledge with the bathwater of formulaic, 'performative' knowledge. In some cases, for example the influential work of Foucault (1980) and many poststructuralists, there is an emphasis on the dangers of social knowledge and its imposing of 'truths' on people and social institutions.[2] Indeed the purpose of a not insignificant part of social science is to warn its readers of the very knowledge of social science, which is sometimes justified but hardly promoting a social science that has anything 'constructive' to offer society. The impression is sometimes that the less social and behavioural knowledge ('dangerous truths') is in circulation, the better.

---

[2] Many warn about the dangers of management and economics knowledge, based on problematic assumptions and creating their self-fulfilling effects, for example transaction cost economics assuming opportunism calling for careful control mechanisms in organizations (Ghoshal, 2005) or studying economics leading to maximization of self-interest (Frank et al., 1993). But it is also relevant to warn against many ideas in psychology, social work, gender studies, sociology, criminology, and education that may be well-intended but express disciplinary and normalizing power, for example through producing 'truths' on justice, human development, gender, ethnic groups, discrimination, and so on. Critique and emancipation may fuel the opposite, as Foucauldians and other poststructuralists often point out.

The chapters that follow examine some of the ways in which meaningless research in social science becomes embedded in different institutions of learning and science, and how individual researchers learn to make sense of their own actions in spite of their fundamental meaninglessness. In particular, we examine the prevailing instrumentalism of social science researchers and its dysfunctional implications.

3

Institutions Encouraging Competition, Instrumentalism, and Meaningless Research

The dominance of formulaic, unimaginative, assumption-reproducing, and largely meaningless research can be observed from different perspectives and with different actors in mind. One can say that this is a systemic effect or that it is an outcome of researchers' collective and individual choices. While renouncing defeatism, we go through how different power structures and career priorities push researchers in certain directions, especially in the direction of easily measurable research outputs in the form of highly-ranked journal articles. We present our analysis at the three customary levels of social science: the micro level of individuals pursuing career success; the meso level of universities wanting position and reputational success; and the macro level of societies eager to gain a competitive advantage as knowledge societies and capitalize on the benefits of commercial innovation. At each level, we establish how competition for status and resources reduces research to instrumentality. We start, however, by putting competition into the broad context of the increased massification of higher education. We end the chapter with a discussion of the role of academics—often misleadingly presented or presenting themselves as victims. We see them (us) as mainly responsible for the sad state of affairs—as researchers, reviewers, editors, supervisors, and in other ways producers and reproducers of dominant academic institutions.

Societal Context: On the Massification of Higher Education

In order to understand the contemporary situation, we need to consider the broader context of universities in a time of mass higher education. The rise of mass higher education is among the most prominent phenomena of our times. Traditionally a mechanism primarily for professional training and for the reproduction of social elites, higher education has exploded to become a core part of contemporary society and part of the life course of virtually all citizens in the developed—and to a growing extent also developing—world. The rapid expansion of higher education has had an immense effect on individuals and groups in society, propelling career expectations and future outlooks. The effects show also at the political level, where education is now widely seen as providing a critical underpinning of national greatness, prosperity, and welfare. The expansion of higher education is closely linked to a political ambition to become a leading knowledge-intensive nation. This tendency is clearly visible in the US—still the dominant global player in higher education—but also in China, where higher education has expanded dramatically since the late 1990s, and in Europe where the unification of European educational systems via the Bologna process, is part of the ambition to foster the 'world's most competitive knowledge-based economy' (as was stated in the 2001 Lisbon strategy).

All this may appear as rational and good. Education is good and the more, the better. But there are reasons to be less sanguine about the common orthodoxy of the virtues of higher education. The strong—arguably almost blind—belief in higher education as a way of increasing economic success, raising the intelligence of the masses, and solving a wide range of societal and individual problems exaggerates the benefits of higher education compared to other forms of learning, including from work practice and networks. One of the major problems afflicting higher education in many different countries is the gradual decline in the quality of learning and the resulting lowering of the value of academic qualifications. With a massive hike in student numbers, an increasing proportion of them start their degrees with weak prior knowledge, no particular aptitude for studying, and are only mildly interested in their disciplines (Arum & Roksa 2011). This places great pressures on teachers faced with exaggerated demands and expectations from the outside world, as well as extreme variations in the range of students they teach: their motivation, competence, and requirements (Comodromos & Gough, 2015; Handal, 2003, p. 18). According to Arum & Roksa (2011), a very large number of students starting higher education studies in the USA are not prepared for it. They cite a survey according to which 40 per cent of the college faculty agrees with the statement 'Most of the students I teach lack the basic skills for college level work' (p. 86). These authors followed 2,200 US students over their college years, using tests designed to investigate critical thinking, analytical reasoning, problem solving, and writing. They found that some 45 per cent of students in the sample had made no effective progress in critical thinking, complex reasoning, and writing in their first two years and 37 per cent did not improve after four years of study when typically ending their programme. According to Arum and Roksa, 'an astounding proportion of students are progressing through higher education today without measurable gains in general skills' (p. 36). Such skills are what higher education institutions broadly emphasize as their major contribution, making contemporary US higher education appear unsuccessful. Those majoring in the liberal arts fields outperformed those studying business, communications, and other practically oriented majors. Nowadays the liberal arts attract a far smaller proportion of students than they did two generations ago. A common complaint among many university teachers is the lack of student motivation. Many commentators stress the low level of motivation and the limited time students spend on their studies (for example Piereson, 2011). According to Arum and Roksa (2011), the majority of students come to university with no particular interest in their courses, and no sense of how these might prepare them for future careers. Many students spend a modest amount of time studying.

There are reasons to be sceptical of the consequences of the expansion of higher education for the university system. The university sector hosts ever increasing numbers of young people into an ever-widening spectrum of education, throughout the world. This is matched by a proliferation in the number of university teachers, who are generally expected to hold a PhD and be active researchers to ensure that teaching is research-based. The number of higher education institutions worldwide is growing rapidly. These all have an interest and a stake in the continuing expansion of higher education and increasingly behave as actors in a market for higher education, peddling their goods as necessary and essential to successful careers, and tailoring working conditions and leadership styles to meet the expectations of their customers. Higher education is 'sold' on the premise of its importance in a knowledge-intensive labour market. Individuals internalize the belief that higher education is the most significant path towards career success. This belief reveals as much as it conceals about the role and function of education in society. Higher education falsely emerges as a win-win game where everybody gains: the individual gets empowered, society becomes more intelligent and richer, while economies move up the value ladder and universities may continue to expand and may continue to recruit ever more university teachers with ever expanding opportunities to cultivate their talents in education and research. But neither the number of competent and motivated graduates and qualified university teachers nor the creation or supply of skilled employment live up to the hype—instead of a mass of high-quality jobs being created, increasing numbers of owners of paper qualifications including PhDs find themselves in menial jobs that make no demands on their qualifications, or seek still higher qualifications in the hope of landing those elusive high-quality and high paying jobs (Sweet & Meiksins, 2008; Wolf, 2004).

Educational fundamentalism, the unquestioned belief that the expansion of higher education is good and will lead to the solutions to all sorts of problems, is a quintessential element of the contemporary phenomenon of grandiosity (Alvesson, 2013a), that is, the large discrepancy between image and substance, where different occupations and professions seek to enhance their status by requiring ever-higher qualifications and vocational training at university level. The accreditation of qualifications over a long period of time is then seen as increasing the income and enhancing the careers of individuals. There is some truth to this. People with a higher degree tend to earn more than those with a shorter education. Education may therefore be viewed as a good investment. Similarly, as people with higher education tend to have a lower unemployment rate and are doing better, it may be argued that higher education functions as a prophylactic against poverty, unemployment, poor health, and other social ills. But the value of education on the labour market is a *positional good* (Alvesson, 2013a; Hirsch, 1976). It is not education per se as its relative position and value vis-à-vis others that matters. People with credentials and qualifications above average tend to benefit more than those below them, not necessarily because their skills are objectively needed for the work they do, but often simply because they occupy a superior position in the economic hierarchy. Turning a very large part of the population into scientists, lawyers, and physicians would lead to a drop in earnings, the job conditions of these professions, and to a steady rise in unemployment for those with lower credentials. Hence, there is a level beyond which more education has a diminishing impact on individuals, economies, and societies. It is mainly those graduating from institutions with a good reputation that get a real payoff from their credentials. This dynamic therefore leads to an intensification in the competition among universities in supplying the positional goods of paper qualifications (Naidoo, 2016). A qualification from university A may thus be worth much more than a superior qualification from a lesser university.

As higher education becomes a mass-market phenomenon, universities are turning from temples of knowledge into factories for the production of credentials. The more universities and the more students who graduate, the lesser the status and market value of an academic qualification. A direct consequence of this is the intensification of competition among universities to establish the status and prestige of their qualifications and attract more and better students. Differentiation becomes a key factor as universities seek to claim unique qualities and attractions (Marginson, 2006). Previously, with fewer universities and students, the dividing line between universities and other institutions able to award qualifications was clear, and distinctions and rankings among universities relatively modest. By contrast, status anxieties and worries are now driving most higher education institutions, in particular where there are official or semi-official publicly available rankings. The rise of ranking agencies has been closely linked to the increasing differentiation among universities and the incessant competition for status in a bid to enhance their qualifications as positional goods. Ranking agencies include universities themselves (for example the widely disseminated Academic Ranking of World Universities (ARWU) compiled by the Shanghai Jiao Tong University); quasi-governmental bodies (like the UKs Higher Education Funding Council for England which oversees the administration of the Research Excellence Framework (REF) ranking of each university department in the country); various newspapers and other publications (like *Forbes, The Financial Times* and *The Times Higher Education*); as well as agencies organized by 'consumers' themselves (like the UK National Union of Students which runs the highly influential National Student Survey). Prospective students and their funders today face a veritable cornucopia of information regarding the merits and reputation of different university offerings, the quality of the teaching provision and college life, and the 'employability' prospects provided by their qualifications.

The growth of rankings and agencies that produce them has been parasitic to the growth of the sector as a whole. Rankings and status are a certain proxy for institutional quality, they provide some information to students in what would otherwise be a chaotic marketplace and they encourage competition among institutions which, at least sometimes, may be of benefit to their 'consumers' and even to society as a whole. But even if rankings lead to some performance improvements, in particular in research, it is not necessarily clear that the quality of education provided to students benefits from this (Sauder & Espeland, 2009). Research orientation and student orientation are often negatively correlated (Arum & Roksa, 2011) and research universities that score highly on the rankings for prestige and reputation are not necessarily the best at offering a sound education to students (Marginson, 2006). The key ability of elite institutions is to maintain and improve their status and position in the rankings by compartmentalizing research and education—producing high-status research with one hand and high-status credentials with the other.

We are not denying that rankings encourage institutions and people to improve and publicize their performance—they are far from purely destructive. Their advantages are obvious: they provide some information to external groups, they offer feedback to those responsible, and exercise some pressure to try to improve. Without any external pressure, academic life can become somewhat laid-back, and a tolerant, laissez-faire attitude is common. But as with every measurement, rankings run the risk of focussing attention to specific metrics (citations, funding revenue, proportion of foreign staff, publications in particular lists of journals, and so on) at the expense of the overall quality of research and education they provide. There is, as Enders (2015) points out, a simplistic but deceptive 'beauty of rankings, and their standardized, de-contextualized, commensurate measures' (p. 163). Competition may improve metrics, not substantive performances. Moreover, position in these rankings is notoriously volatile as tiny changes in the scores or the measurement methods can lead to big drops or rises in the rankings. Thus, an announced drop of both Oxford and Cambridge universities by two places in reputational rankings over the previous year (2015) can be accorded far more significance than it merits, sparking deep self-questioning. Similarly, Beijing University's 'leap' of eleven places in the same year to attain the twenty-first place can be interpreted as representing a 'massive surge' in the quality of 'Asian universities'. Such ephemeral changes over a single year can prompt a reputable professor of higher education to be quoted saying 'We've had a highly Anglo-Saxon view of higher education for many years, and that can't be sustained for much longer', a pronouncement that may be accurate but hardly warranted by the results of a single ranking survey (especially when the same survey in the previous year had extolled 'a strong performance from the UK and France—nations which have increased their share of the world's most-renowned universities').

If rankings encourage 'gaming' among academics and their institutions, this is also true for students and graduates. Several universities have been accused of putting pressure on their students, in order to give high scores to their universities' courses in the UK's National Student Survey, otherwise they risk undermining the value of their degree and their prospects of employment. This practice may be limited to a few institutions, but students' awareness that low scores deflate their qualifications and employability is widespread in the UK higher education sector, calling into question the validity and reliability of the rankings as well as some of their ethical premises.

Status Competition at Different Levels and the Proliferation of Published Research

The massification of higher education reinforces zero-sum or even winner-takes-all games centring on status and reputation. With the expansion of the sector, the declining value of qualifications, and falling standards of education, the overall status of the sector and the self-esteem of those working in it drops. A few decades ago a university was a prestigious institution and university lecturers were ranked high on the status ladders in most countries. With this a certain identity, self-esteem, and self-confidence followed. Competition among scholars undoubtedly was common but it lacked the intensity and desperation that it currently engenders in many settings, where most academics are struggling to enhance their status as researchers, to avoid institutions with poorly prepared, unmotivated and consumer-oriented students, and to reduce their teaching as much as possible. There is thus a twin

41

effect of teaching both decreasing in status and becoming less intrinsically motivating. The two elements reinforce each other. Increased efforts on research are visible, easily measurable attainments, with notable 'hits' in prestigious journals becoming central. There is thus a rush to research as means of escaping the mass education trap. Faculty members with a strong research record find it easier to escape large introductory courses with large volumes of soul-destroying marking and find more attractive elective courses with fewer and more interested students—although factory-like first year courses may also affect the initially more interested students negatively so the more appealing parts of education may be further reduced. Research emerges as a status booster of considerable significance as university teaching becomes less prestigious and impoverished. Reduced resources per student in many institutions (reflected, for instance in time allowed for lecture preparation or marking) compound to make teaching even less attractive. While the sector is dragged forward by mass education and the craving for formal qualifications, the reputation of universities and of individual academics is won on the back of research successes. But competition for status and position in research is harsh. We can see this on three different levels.

Micro level: researchers competing for jobs and promotion. With the advent of mass education there are more aspiring researchers than ever, although the ratio of aspirants and positions are unevenly distributed across social science. Since it is impossible for all to have tenured positions in high-status institutions (indeed, there are good reasons for this), some form of performance measure is necessary. The sheer volume of academics and writings means that qualitative assessment gives way to metrics, including the counting of articles in highly-ranked journals and bibliometric impact indices. Audits may be decoupled from the actual work they seek to monitor, or actively colonize it in the sense that the work is amended to score high on the audit's parameters. In social science, there appears to be considerably more colonizing than decoupling, as many of the players take performance measures very seriously and adapt their actions accordingly (Sauder & Espeland, 2009). The benefits generated by actual published articles often take precedence over active participation in discussions, generation of good ideas, creativity, brightness, and potential. What is tangible and easy to assess takes precedence over more unquantifiable qualities and results in more tangible rewards.

Meso level: universities competing for position. As mentioned, mass education, the increasing commodification of higher education, and the rising dominance of market mechanisms in the delivery of its services has led to hitherto unprecedented competition not only among researchers but also among universities, and to an attendant proliferation of rankings. Departments, faculties, and universities are ceaselessly ranked according to how well they collectively score on various indices. This leads, as we saw earlier, to a pecking order of reputations and standings that are crucial for attracting students as well as research funds (Marginson, 2006; Naidoo, 2016). This is not in itself a problem—competition at departmental and university level can lead to quality improvements. Laissez-faire cultures can be shaken up and institutions more or less forced to monitor how they use resources and refrain from inbreeding and nepotism. The problem is the one-dimensionality and the mechanics of the competition. However, when success in the competition depends on pumping out as many outputs in the right journals as possible (themselves liable to constant rankings and competition), and these tend to become increasingly similar and formulaic, the quality of scholarship and education becomes distorted and social relevance marginalized. Competition based on learning and the increase of students' qualification as well as really significant and meaningful research results would be good, but is hardly what rankings measure.

Macro level: governments striving after legitimacy, international standing, and voters. In the so-called 'knowledge society', science takes on a symbolic value as a measure of the success of different nations. Nations are eager that their universities emerge at the top of international rankings and that their graduates are even more numerous and more qualified than those of other countries. Science and knowledge are supposed to be the breeding ground for innovators who, every now and then, come up with new inventions, creating new industries and employment opportunities. Higher education is supposed to lead to the good life for as many as possible, and here research is often presented as a guarantee for the quality of lecturers and teaching. Sometimes things do work in this way. However, research is often no more than a source of legitimation for the supposed quality of higher education, and may cover up the decline in standards of service delivered to students or the contribution of social research to society. This falls under the radar, as governments are evaluated according to how well they have promoted 'science' in their respective nations. The sheer volume and ambiguity of research make qualified assessment difficult. In these evaluation, the same metrics as those for evaluating universities and individual researchers are employed.

A fundamental consequence of all this intensified competition at different levels is a radical disconnection between the astronomical volume of research papers that act as the tools for the competition, and the social relevance and meaning of this material. Mass education has been accompanied by mass research and mass publication. Given how much has already been written over the years on almost any possible topic, there is a decreasing number of academic projects that are truly innovative, valuable, or relevant, and thus readership is rapidly declining. The purpose of research publications is now firmly tied to employability, promotion, status, and legitimation for individuals, an escape route from too much teaching, and enhanced rankings for their departments rather than raising the knowledge and intellectual level of society. It is therefore not surprising that, at least in social science, the proportion of novel, socially relevant knowledge is decreasing or getting lost in the noise of overproduction. The resulting meaninglessness of research publications is easily covered up by seemingly impressive metrics seducing people to believe that having more papers in the right journals or high citation scores are the same as quality and contribution to the social good. Meaning and social value become secondary, as status and position become the burning issues for everybody involved—individuals, institutions, societies—desperate to climb the ladder and score as high as possible. Eager to climb up the rankings, many university departments are currently hiring and promoting academics purely on the strength of their journal publications lists, with little concern for the content of these publications or, for that matter, the other scholarly or scientific credentials of these appointments. The result is the emergence of a super-elite of star academics, able to play the labour market to their benefit, moving across institutions for ever increasing rewards, not unlike star footballers, against a backcloth of dropping standards and declining status and conditions of work for the majority of other academics employed in the sector.

Still, one could ask, what is the problem with large quantities of research and a wealth of publications? Why not let a thousand flowers bloom? Even if not all of them are outstanding, it may be argued that even modest contributions enable researchers to develop their skills and maybe offer better contributions in future. Besides, why not accept that a plethora of minor works are the necessary price to pay for a few significant ones to emerge? And who can with certainty tell what is really good and valuable and what is not? These are valid concerns, but it is not a responsible attitude to simply prescribe the expansion of resources for research time and publications. There are other, sometimes more pressing needs outside or within universities competing with research. As we have noted, the explosion of research efforts and paper production is very costly in terms of attention, priority, and time by the university lecturers. Time and resources spent on research are at the expense of other activities. Allocation of huge resources for research may be good for (some) academics, but it is doubtful if it is good for society. Do we, as a society, need or benefit from all this research? Benefits may often be uncertain or questionable and may not outweigh costs and disadvantages of which we have singled out three:

1. Resources devoted to academic research means fewer resources allocated to other social purposes (nurseries, schools, old age care, and so on) and/or higher costs to taxpayers and students.

2. Resources devoted by universities to research are denied to teaching, which consequently loses in reputation and prestige and thus attention to and care of education.

3. Proliferation of publications leads to ever-higher specialization, to the isolation of researchers within their microtribes, and to increasing noise which makes it hard for genuinely innovative work to get heard.

There are good reasons to assume, as Grey and Sinclair (2006) state, that we are publishing too much. We will return to this issue.

Institutional Conditions: Journal Publication Logics and Professional Norms

In addition to the rapid rise of mass higher education, the increasing competition among academics, universities, and nations and the emergence of various ranking agencies, a major institutional contributor to the current proliferation of meaningless research are academic journals, their publishers, editors, and editorial boards. Faced with demands to evaluate research performance prior to allocating funding, research funding bodies across the globe are increasingly governed by various grading processes, such as RAE/REF (Research Assessment Exercise/Research Excellence Framework) in the UK and ERA (Excellence in Research in Australia) in Australia. A key performance indicator in those processes is the number of articles published in high-ranking journals within *designated journal lists*. This has meant that practically the only research outputs that count in departments of prestigious universities are publications in A-listed journals. Other institutions try to mimic this example, even though also B-journals are here relevant and acknowledged. As noted by many across the entire scientific field (for example Adler & Harzing, 2009; Lawrence, 2008), the use of such lists encourages researchers to concentrate on publishing articles in particular journals rather than trying to develop more original knowledge. In management studies, Macdonald and Kam (2007, p. 702) observed that: 'All but forgotten in the desperation to win the game is publication as a means of communicating research findings for the public benefit.' And even in natural science, Lawrence (2008, p. 1) noted that the use of journal lists for evaluating academic research performance has meant that 'scientists have been forced to down-grade their primary aim of making discoveries to publishing as many papers as possible'. This implies that the competition for position among academic institutions and individual researchers leads into negative effects on knowledge development, and that socially meaningful research is not prioritized, as academics are disciplined by often conservative and mainstreaming journal publication regimes.

The pressure to publish in highly-ranked journals does not of itself reduce innovative work—to some extent it favours it—but as we will discuss below, the ways in which these journals are run encourages incremental research rather than radical innovation and intellectual boldness. Journals, editors, and reviewers are the main professional norm setters for how research is conducted, and the gatekeepers of what research gets published. Incremental research is strongly encouraged by the *'adding-to-the literature'* norm within leading journals as the primary evidence for research contribution. For example, based on her twenty-six years as *Administrative Science Quarterly*'s managing editor and her reading of more than 19,000 reviews and more than 8,000 decision letters, Johanson (2007, p. 292) firmly advises authors to adhere to the adding-to-the literature norm because 'if you can't make a convincing argument that you are filling an important gap in the literature, you will have a hard time establishing that you have a contribution to make to that literature'. The prevalence of the adding-to-the-literature norm is also evident in Miller et al.'s (2009, p. 278) observation that our top-tier journals increasingly force researchers into incremental research as they 'encourage work on topics that fit neatly within today's popular theories and allow the development and tweaking of those theories'. Similarly, in a recent special issue on theory development, the guest editor argued that '[i]n the interest of theory development, management and organizational research would make better progress if we devoted more attention to theoretical refinement, conducting research that identifies the boundaries and limitations of theories, stages competitive tests between rival theories, and increases the precision of theories so they yield strong predictions that can be falsified' (Edwards, 2010, p. 615).

This emphasis on applying and polishing theory—rather than trying to say something original and meaningful—is common across many social science disciplines, including education, management, psychology, and sociology (Alvesson & Sandberg, 2013). The strong adding-to-the-literature norm in many social science journals does not necessarily mean that challenging dominant assumptions or developing more novel ideas is directly discouraged. One often hears calls for more provocative, challenging work, not least from editors themselves. However, the insistence on carefully relating any piece of study to existing literature tends to encourage researchers to look for gaps, and not to move very far from an established body of work in their specific subfield. More subversive and consensus-challenging work which may draw inspiration from outside a (sub)field and break away from the incremental norm is seen as risky and potentially damaging for careers, and is viewed as the prerogative of scholars with well-established reputations.

The demand to meticulously relate one's study to existing literature is also underpinned by a specific kind of *rigour* upheld by many journals, their reviewers, and editors. It typically requires (a) a systematic and overly pedantic vacuum cleaning of existing literature, as a way of demonstrating how one's own study contributes to existing literature; and (b) an emphasis on detailed codification procedures or statistical techniques carried out on any empirical material without asking whether there is anything fundamentally problematic with existing literature, or whether the data really addresses the phenomena under investigation. As the outgoing editors of a journal observed in their final editorial note: 'The emphasis on improving the rigour of theorizing and of empirical method . . . may have led to more incremental research questions being addressed' (Clark & Wright, 2009, p. 6).

Incremental research is further encouraged by the increasing tendency among academics to *pigeonhole* themselves (and their subject matter) into narrow and well-mastered areas. Such pigeonholing helps to boost their productivity and to meet academic performance criteria in the sense that: one knows the literature, goes to the right conferences, cultivates a network of peers that matters, is familiar with the norms and rules of the journals in the sub-area, and therefore is capable of successfully publishing incremental contributions regularly. But the likelihood of generating original research through such pigeonholing is low, as basic assumptions and established wisdom are taken for granted and reproduced. In particular, many reviewers and editors expect authors to cite a significant part of the work in a particular subfield, including a substantial number of their own publications or ones published in their journal. By the same token, they often show limited energy, interest, and tolerance for theories and ideas originating outside their subfield as a way of opening up new areas of inquiry (Alvesson & Sandberg, 2014; Starbuck, 2003).

Incremental research is also promoted by the strongly held *accumulation* norm in social science that knowledge is supposed to advance through incremental accumulation within a particular field. For example, in its criteria for publication, the *Academy of Management Journal* stipulates that 'submissions should clearly communicate the nature of their theoretical contribution in relation to the existing management and organizational literatures'. Similarly, the *Journal of Management Studies* says that its main criterion for publication is that a submitted paper should contribute 'significantly to the development of coherent bodies of knowledge'. The accumulation norm tends to reinforce the incremental logic by requiring researchers to adopt a systematic, analytical, and often narrow focus, which makes them unable to ask more fundamental and sceptical questions that may encourage some significant rethinking of the subject matter in question. This accumulation norm also aims at creating an impression of a collective project guided by rationality and aimed at gradual progress, which works as an antidote to a lurking feeling that much social research is guided by subjectivity, arbitrariness, and relativism (Pfeffer, 1993). Hence, the incremental approach may be used to legitimate not only individual pieces of research, but also the scientific project itself, as a process of piecemeal and incremental accumulation of knowledge against the contrary arguments of Kuhn (1970) and others (Burrell & Morgan, 1979; Delanty, 2005), emphasizing the role of paradigmatic assumptions, and pointing at the possibility that problematic assumptions may lead to problematic results, and thus undermining the idea that building upon and adding to earlier knowledge automatically means progress.

Journals and their procedures function as a strong disciplinary regime—as such they are a mixed blessing. There is certainly value in rejecting poor papers containing no novel ideas or other contributions to knowledge with no regard for the reputation of their authors. Most published articles clearly benefit from some revisions undertaken as part of the review process. But increasingly the review process can be counterproductive. Original ideas, independent thinking, and projects of social importance are curtailed by the demand to ground everything in 'existing literature' in a specific subfield and by constant revisions aimed at satisfying the requirements of different reviewers. As Gabriel (2010, p. 764) observed:

> Publishing is now a long process, involving numerous revisions, citing authors one does not care for, engaging with arguments one is not interested in and seeking to satisfy different harsh masters, often with conflicting or incompatible demands, while staying within a strict word limit. Most authors will go through these tribulations and the drudgery of copious revisions, accepting virtually any criticism and any recommendation with scarcely any complaint, all in the interest of getting published.

Overall then we would argue that the review process, while ensuring a minimum of quality in a formal sense and preventing overt favouritism, has a conservative effect on research publications, flattening out much that would be controversial, subjective, uncomfortable, or disturbing for an existing order of a microtribe. The problem, according to our experience, is less about good papers being rejected by journals, than researchers adapting to expectations of the publishing regime and mainstreaming themselves within established frameworks, and not doing sufficiently ambitious and creative groundwork to writing potentially promising papers.

Academics: Victims or in Charge?

This and the previous chapter have examined different forces and institutions that account for what we view as a dangerous depletion of meaning in social science research.[1] This includes the growth of mass higher education, the

---

[1] This section draws upon Alvesson & Sandberg (2013).

increasing competition at all levels, the rise of rankings and ranking agencies, the growing instrumentality governing researchers engaged in the publishing game, and the part played by academic journals themselves. We have also indicated the numerous discontents that arise from the current system and the costs that taxpayers, students, and their funders are asked to bear. In concluding this chapter, we examine the part played by academic researchers themselves in sustaining this system. It is they after all who produce what we have referred to as meaningless research. We also try to assess who benefits from it, and to propose two lines of interpretation.

The victim-of-the-system explanation. It is possible to see the interplay between institutional conditions, professional norms, and the researchers' own identities *as researchers* as a tight system from which it is difficult to break. This emphasizes the connections and mutually reinforcing effects of the three key drivers behind the prevalence of incremental, increasingly meaningless research. Institutions compete for their position in the rankings, journals compete to enter the A-lists and enhance their impact factors, and individual researchers eager to be successful (otherwise facing material and symbolic consequences) strive to enhance their individual scores in the game of publication hits and citations. Researchers derive their identities and self-esteem from their success in this game and will endure many disappointments and privations to enhance their chances of success. Thus, the identity projects (and narcissism) of researchers reinforce the effects of instrumental pressures and material incentives. Individual researchers, like journals and universities, find themselves increasingly caught up in a competition in the rankings and differentiations: to be a good academic means to publish in A-listed journals and do whatever it takes to get published in these journals, which includes specialization and alignment to a specific research microtribe.

In such a tightly regulated system, most researchers would find it inconceivable to spend several years writing a really innovative book. Instead, they are furiously trying to publish in A-listed journals, whose grip over their time, focus, and selfhood is being reinforced. Performing less well in this one-dimensional scale means jeopardizing their academic career possibilities—and perhaps their egos. Many struggle to meet even a modest level of success. Without a steady flow of journal publications, tenure and promotion are jeopardized, teaching loads are likely to increase, money for conferences and books will dry up, and a researcher faces what seems like a nightmare scenario—spending the rest of his or her days in precarious employment, teaching and marking for hundreds of first year undergraduates, and with no prospect of escape from the academic precariat. In order to avoid this scenario, a researcher in such a tightly regulated system will do anything, including engaging in formulaic and meaningless work, in order to enhance the chances of publication.

This 'victim-of-the-system' explanation of meaningless research makes some sense. It is surprising how few protests there have been against this 'evil' system, how little resistance, despite frequent complaints (Alvesson & Spicer, 2016; Clarke & Knights, 2015; Giroux, 2006; Ryan, 2012). The situation persists, even if it is seen as undesirable, through more or less voluntary cooperation and overt or tacit support. There are some people that clearly benefit from the situation. It is not just the winners of the game who are reluctant to change but many of the losers too who sincerely hope that, with a bit of perseverance and skill, they too can become winners. In social science disciplines, it seems that everyone aspires to be a winner in a game they know and understand well by moving to the successful end of the scale. The system provides deans, at least at research-oriented and reasonably successful schools, with a powerful tool to control and monitor the research performance of faculty. Leading journals receive increased submissions and status through high-impact factors. The careers of star researchers flourish. PhD students get clear guidelines how to progress their careers and can be inspired by numerous, but homogenous role models.

The strongest winners are probably researchers highly skilled in neo-positivistic research with sophisticated quantitative, statistical, and modelling skills, whose habitus is geared to journal publication. The use of the conventional journal format fits nicely with their method and mindset. A standardized format, map-and-fill-the-gap, and aim for knowledge accumulation by positively adding to earlier work without too many complications, are important features of such a research paradigm. Other traditions, like rich ethnographic studies, interpretive approaches, reflexive and essayistic contributions, as well as original theoretical ideas do not find such a hospitable home in starred journals; many of them also are not easily packed into the 8,000–10,000 words format, and the less rule-bound types of research make assessments difficult and varied. This type of research takes far longer to conduct, calls for more careful interpretation and the use of language, and lends itself to more challenges and questioning from potential reviewers. It is doubtful if most of the great contributions of social science during the twentieth century would have managed to get published in contemporary academic journals.

The we-are-in-charge-of-the-system explanation. Above, we made a case for how the three ingredients (institutional conditions, professional norms, and researchers' identities) can be seen as a tightly coupled system forcing social science researchers (as victims or beneficiaries) into incremental and largely meaningless research. But one can also argue for a less deterministic view and a looser connection between the three ingredients. Governments and central university administrations are not particularly preoccupied with the specific content and ethos of research undertaken under their auspices. In fact, they would probably applaud great innovations and socially relevant findings with wide-ranging policy and social impact. Above all, they are concerned with claiming that they are getting and offering value for money, that they support a rational allocation of resources, spending wisely taxpayers' money and student fees.

If researchers decided to alter their approach towards more meaningful and socially relevant work, this would not in itself go against regulatory bodies' need to demonstrate that resources are spent in a reasonable way, nor would it inhibit indicators of how well various universities, schools, and research groups are performing. In the UK, for example, the research assessment panels are made up of academics, who have high discretion in how they evaluate different institutional claims. Similarly, journal editors have extensive discretion about the publication policies of their journal. It is sometimes perverse to hear them complain about the articles they publish when they could very well implement policies that encourage imaginative, meaningful, and socially useful studies. Journal review processes may also further reinforce formulaic research, or suggest something quite different, when reviewers recommend acceptance, rejection, or radical revisions of papers.

Most researchers themselves have more discretion than they imagine on how to shape their career, on how to spend their time, and what avenues of inquiry to follow. For example, not all researchers are striving to get tenure at very prestigious universities. Even those who do are only victims of 'whatever it takes' for the period before tenure—besides, they can usually move to another institution with less stringent requirements. Many research active academics have de facto stable jobs for most of their working life with more or less guaranteed time for research in their contracts. Some researchers are also diligent and gifted enough to reach the minimum number of publications required by their departments and can afford to spend the rest of their time on more innovative projects. And experienced researchers who find elite institutions making unreasonable demands on the kinds of publications and research they should be carrying out can, and sometimes do, choose to move to institutions that afford them more freedom and space. Some social science academics can and do stand up for their values and priorities, accepting less than optimal pay, status, and prestige in return for greater fulfilment in the work they do. The good book with an original idea and rich empirical material is also likely to be broadly celebrated and raise a person's standing and career far above the average. In the majority of all cases, competent and ambitious researchers insisting on sound priorities would not face any actual disciplinary consequences other than in their imagination.

One could also reverse the top-down logic and argue that it is *not* institutional arrangements—rankings, funding, performance pressure from the top—that drives the process downwards, but that it works the opposite way. Individuals and collectives—not natural laws or free-floating systems—construct their (our) institutions. It is academics—through their choices and priorities—that establish and revise norms of good research, run journals (as authors, reviewers, editors, members of associations running the journals and of review panels), and socialize young researchers. The latter far too often choose the easy, risk-minimizing way and mimic established templates rather than aiming for originality and independence. This is may be understandable for 'weak' or uncertain persons in an early career stage, and perhaps for some persons in very conformist disciplines, heavily dominated by neo-positivism, but is hardly satisfying for the majority of all in academia across social science. It could then be argued that it is they (we), academics who have the strongest impact on where universities and professional institutions focus their research, how they assign resources, and how they evaluate the quality of different outputs. Researchers, individually and collectively, are in significant ways in charge of how research is conducted and can decide what research counts as valuable, what should be funded, and what should be published. The major problem can hardly be, as one often hears, that those doing the research are good and those who evaluate it are not, since authors, reviewers, editors, members of assessment panels, and funding bodies are all drawn from the same pool of academics. The academic community forms its journals, rather than the other way around—although there is also a loop from journals to community.

As an occupational group, we are substantially exercising collective control over ourselves, voluntarily building our own constraining (and seductive) rules and norms, and willingly giving up a lot of possible discretion (cf. Barker, 1993). After all, who produces the research texts? Who spends so much time and other resources and has so little of real value to show? Who gives feedback and makes recommendations and decisions on what papers and books should be published? We all do—not only senior academics but also younger people undertake reviews and make a difference in acceptance/rejections/forming decisions. As a collective, we substantially control the norms of what counts as good research and, thus, to a considerable degree, form, bend, and translate how governments and other institutions' policies influence the research practice.

There are of course limits to our discretion, notably that the institutional logics of academia are trapped within the frames of neo-liberal capitalism, and there is a complex structure–agency interaction involved that accounts for the fact that institutional arrangements have strong reproductive tendencies and established rules of the game are not easy to change from above or below. We are partly victims of the prisons we (as a large collective) have ourselves built. But institutional policies in themselves do *not* proscribe imaginative, meaningful, and consensus-challenging research. Nor is this work necessarily more time-consuming than formulaic studies devoid of meaning. It does, however, call for different skills and mental habits from the ones we currently encourage.

What above all the 'we-are-in-charge-of-the-system' explanation suggests is that we as researchers have more control than we realize and that there are ample opportunities to put social science research back on track again. This is the line of argument that we will pursue in Part II of this book. Our point here is not to debate whether 'the system' or academics themselves should carry the heavy burden of guilt for the bad state of the art and for initiating change. Most likely there are instances where structure outperforms agency, leaving few opportunities for reform and innovation. There are also, however, instances when academics almost unnecessarily create their own prisons in which they entrap themselves and their colleagues. They then passively wait and accept the prison-like arrangements with little opposition. As a UK professor interviewed by Knights & Clarke (2014, p. 347) said:

> One of my complaints . . . is the extent to which academics are so bloody supine in the face of so much stuff that is pushed upon them.

Behind the 'victim-of-the-system' explanation, there is often an assumption of rigid norms and constraints that produces an excuse for compliance and opportunism. There is also a strong responsiveness to rewards. Assessments like REF appear often to be used by UK researchers as a way to escape responsibility for research that lacks meaning. 'If it were not for the system's constraints, I'd be able to do really great work', is a popular fantasy, protecting self-esteem while occasionally undoubtedly also containing grains of truth. Sometimes absurdities are presented as absolute truths—like that 'you have to publish in US A-journals', which is patently wrong since the great majority of European (and most US) social researchers will never do that (partly because of limited publication space in these journals), and if this injunction was to be taken seriously most social science departments in Europe would be more or less empty or only occupied by temporarily employed lecturers. Developing and reinforcing myths about the impossibility or enormous costs of not following the system's imperatives and rewards/sanctions means that researchers can wash their hands of responsibility, happily complaining about lack of choices, and often profiting from the game. Rumours and concrete examples about individuals failing to get tenure, facing delayed promotion, or being put on teaching-only contracts are often anecdotally mentioned in conversations, but the greater number of instances when individuals get and keep their jobs despite poor research performances are seldom discussed.

The average hired or tenured lecturer or professor in most social science departments is a moderately qualified person. In certain disciplines, in certain countries and in certain times, it may be difficult to get employment, in particular at highly-ranked institutions. Generally, however, in an age of mass higher education, getting an academic job is considerably less daunting than at most earlier times.

Conclusion

In this chapter we have addressed policy and institutional issues of relevance for the lack of meaning in contemporary social science. It would be a mistake to see journal publication regimes solely as drivers of meaninglessness. The principle that researchers must not only satisfy the opinions of their local or national peers but need to face international peer review and competition often fosters better research and leads to valuable knowledge contributions. But unfortunately there are very strong signs of formulaic, instrumental, and cautious studies dominating the field, and that the requirement to satisfy reviewers and get published takes upper hand.

One can understand this as an outcome of system pressures associated with international trends, national and university policies, and a scientific apparatus geared to producing positive outcomes in terms of rankings and numbers. One must, however, also emphasize how academics individually and collectively contribute to this—as researchers, supervisors, advice givers, reviewers, and editors. We believe that academics are both victims of the system and key operators in charge of forming research. They are sometimes prone to self-victimization, i.e. eager to adopt a position of 'no choice', rationalization compliance, and work of limited value. To act wisely and responsibly calls for reflection in a variety of ways. Without being naïve about voluntarism and agency, we must consider seriously our roles as researchers and the scope that these give us to conduct meaningful and socially relevant research. This is central for research and contributions and also the key to affect the institutions that then go on to affect researchers and research. Individual reviewers can start this process by asking serious questions about how meaningful and socially valuable is a research project or a paper, and to ask for more of this. But surely changes are needed also on macro levels. We will present our own ideas about this as well as about changes at the policy and institutional levels in Part II of the book.

4

Researchers Making Sense of Meaningless Research

Whenever the discontents of 'publish and/or perish' are aired, researchers appear remarkably feeble, almost like marionettes in a puppet show gone awry. As we noted in the previous chapters, there are many institutional pressures encouraging researchers in the direction of meaningless research; we also argued, however, that many of us enjoy considerable freedoms; freedoms that would baffle the majority of the working population. We can choose what to study, where and when to study it, who we collaborate with, what conferences we attend, what we read, and what we write. As social scientists, we are aware that institutional structures can only be maintained as long as the institutional members adapt to them. Voice and exit prompt change (Hirschman, 1970), even if deafness to critique and the exchangeability of people limit the effects. Even if much of what takes place in universities is entangled with larger socio-political developments, most academics are still able to shape the academic assessment systems and at least minimize the perversions they engender. As Martin Parker puts it in an openhearted reflection on his time as an editor at the journal *Organization*: 'even if you take the global capitalists out of the process, the rest of the set up stays the same. That is to say that states, universities as competitors and employers, academics and (perhaps most importantly) ranking entrepreneurs will generally continue to operate' (Parker, 2013, p. 472).

Even Marxists would find it hard to attribute all the problems that afflict contemporary universities to capitalist production forces. The inanities of research assessment exercises, journal lists, and departmental rankings are largely self-inflicted, as are most of the perverse outcomes of social research projects, academic reviews, and journal publications. So too are many of the abstruse canons governing academic promotions and probations, the silos that prevent knowledge from being shared or tested across disciplines, the style of expression that has now become established as 'academic writing', and the fetishizing of impact factors and citations. In *Learn to Write Badly,* Michael Billig (2013, p. 153) contends: ' "Citation statistics" have not come from outside the academic world as if an alien imposition, but we academics have created the means by which we govern ourselves.' We have full responsibility to use them—mechanically or selectively and wisely—or to refrain from using them.

The question then becomes *why* we have created this system and how can we tolerate it in spite of the constant complaints and whingeing, and the realization that such a system serves neither the generation of meaningful knowledge nor the meaningful education of our students. Billig emphasizes the compelling nature of assessment systems that now dominate the academic mindset: 'to do our jobs successfully, we need to acquire a fundamental academic skill that the scholars of old generally did not possess: modern academics must be able to keep writing and publishing even when they have nothing to say' (Billig, 2013, p. 26). Individual researchers find it impossible to escape from this straightjacket of constant writing in order to get published, disciplining themselves against all the odds to keep finding things they can write about. Quantity obliterates quality. There is often a strong feeling that each academic is only worth as much as his/her last publication and must constantly keep on the move. This proliferation of academic texts inevitably leads to saturation—how is one to recognize what is valuable in the midst of a profusion of texts by authors who have nothing to say, but are experts in concealing it?

Here, too, quantity comes to take the part of quality. The impact factor of the journal or, better, the number of citations comes to be experienced as a mark of quality. The publication turns into a citation game, every bit as ugly, competitive and meaningless:

> I am pleased if I am mentioned in more articles than they are, and my mood will be spoiled if their numbers surpass mine. It is as if I am pathetically pleading with the academic world: 'Please, please mention me; you only need mention me in passing; just drop my name; I don't care where or how; just mention me, please; oh, and don't bother mentioning Dr X or Professor Y.' Do I really think like this? Do I really care about the numbers? Yes, I must do. What a knob head.
>
> (Billig, 2013, p. 155)

What is unusual in Billig is his candour, not his experience. He is far from alone in being seized by this bean-counting mentality where one's worth as a scholar or even one's standing as a human being amounts to the number of times one has been cited, often by people who have not read the work and care little about it. Why then do we find ourselves writing things even when we do not have very much to say? Why do we write things that we know will probably not be read by anyone and not make any impressions in terms of offering valuable insights or information? Is it only a matter of getting published or making a career? Does a logic of adding items to a CV publications list explain it all?

In Billig's and most others' accounts there is a strong element of 'must', but as Billig also emphasizes, there are strong elements of feelings and beliefs involved. Behind the 'must' there is a construction, or as Billig writes, 'our worries drive us'. That an academic is only as good as his/her last publication is perhaps mainly a reflection of the lack of publications that have any enduring quality. Most of us have true and deep respect for the author of a good book or article even if it appeared some time ago, but such authors are relatively few today in social science. Our impression—based on our own observations and numerous conversations with others—is that there are fewer and fewer contributions that are clearly noticed and stand out as worthy of broad attention.

We are not denying that many social science researchers at least some of the time do valuable and meaningful work. What we are contending, however, is that much of this work is not suitable for publication and readership or—at best—offers little of value to anyone outside the researcher's microtribe or to society at large. When looking closely at academic 'knob-head-behaviour', we notice several types of self-justification to the increasing irrelevance of what we write. In this chapter, we present the most common types of adaptive rationales that have been reported in studies on academic researchers (for example Clarke & Knights, 2015; Knights & Clarke, 2014), observed among colleagues and, following some critical self-reflection, in ourselves. Each of these rationales represents a mode of creating meaning for what is largely a meaningless activity; a rationalization for what is undoubtedly pretty meaningless but highly demanding work.

These rationales can be ordered along two spectra (see Figure 4.1). The instrumentalism-narcissism-spectrum refers to whether individual researchers are directed at satisfying the needs of their own egos or at satisfying the external set of criteria and requirements to get research grants, papers accepted for publication, and jobs and promotion—even in those (many) cases where this means adapting to what you do not believe in. The religiosity-cynicism-spectrum refers to whether researchers bring themselves to believe that they are contributing to science as a great and noble enterprise, or whether they dismiss such ambitions as illusory. The adaptive rationales can be found between these extremes as illustrated in Figure 4.1. It should be noted that these are ideal-typical rationales that help individual researchers engage in what appears meaningless to themselves and/or to others. A single individual may embrace several of these rationales at the same time or may adopt different ones over time. We don't claim that the rationales are empirically accurate—the idea is not so much to map motivational realities as much as to provide ideas and vocabulary for critical thinking and communication.

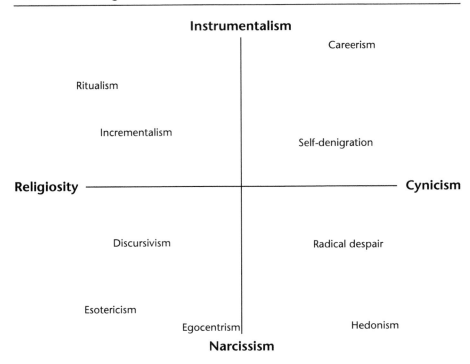

Figure 4.1. Adaptive rationales between the extremes of religiosity, narcissism, cynicism, and instrumentalism

Starting in the upper-left corner, the adaptive rationales can be summarized as follows.

'I am a real researcher': Scientific Ritualism

This rationale is based on an almost religious sense of honour at belonging to the scientific community. Writing in this capacity gives researchers their authority, making their work more 'real'. Proud to belong to the fraternity, ritualists are not troubled by the fact that what they write is of no interest to the general public or even to those closely associated with professional fields in which research is conducted. Rather, they are preoccupied with being as scientific as possible as a means to gain entry into what they view as an elite, thus assuring their identity. First and foremost, they seek to publish articles in top-ranked journals. Packaging knowledge into texts of 8,000–10,000 words in a way which satisfies editors and reviewers, represents their greatest ambition. As reviewers, scientific ritualists are experts in a subfield, aware of its tiniest conventions and rigorous in their observance. The formulae for what is viewed as good research are strictly upheld. For example, a ritualist is inclined to demand that the author demonstrate how coding was conducted without considering whether coding is a good way of dealing with data, as this denies ambiguity, context and fragments material, as well as encouraging superficial aspects, and reduces the chances for rich and imaginative interpretations. (There is much critique of the coding ideal, for example, Potter & Wetherell, 1987). Rigid and unimaginative, ritualists prevent others from what may be viewed as novel and imaginative work outside the narrow box of their expertise (Alvesson & Sandberg, 2014). As the ability to recognize relevance decreases, so the ritualists' feeling for errors and omissions in trivia of theory or methodology increases. This emphasis on 'rigour' is not new. It was once described by Adorno as a 'sickness' of the researchers' intellectual powers, a way of avoiding thinking that 'burdens them with a subjective responsibility which their objective position in the production process does not allow them to meet'. Many are perfectly aware of this 'sickness', argued Adorno, but 'they all find it publicly acclaimed as a moral achievement, and see themselves recognized for a scientific asceticism which to them is none, but the secret contour of their weakness' (Adorno, 2005 [1951], p. 124). To the ritualist, minor infringements and omissions in matters of methodology, existing literature, and even academic etiquette constitute moral sins. In all these ways, scientific ritualists are obsessed with what the rest of society views as 'purely academic' issues.

In public contexts, the ritualist likes to say: 'we ought to pay more attention to *real scientific* research'.

'I am a part of a far greater whole': Incrementalism

Religious panentheism approaches every aspect of the universe as constituted by a divinity greater than the sum of its parts, whose purposes are unknown and unknowable. In a similar way, scientific incrementalists believe that what they write is part of a whole which is beyond comprehension. The whole can be both spatial and temporal. Incrementalists may acknowledge that their own contribution appears to be insignificant, but they imagine it to be of momentous importance to researchers in other parts of the world. As part of the enormous kingdom of science, the full relevance and importance of their work will be revealed at some point in the future. As soon as enough pieces of the puzzle have been added, a larger picture will emerge at which point science will take a step forward and their own contribution will be recognized. For the incrementalist, the sea of texts which are forgotten as quickly as they are produced is further evidence of the greatness of science, and 'publish or perish' is welcomed as evidence of the greatness of the enterprise of which they are part. Given the enormous popularity of 'gap-spotting'—find and fill a hole in the literature—incrementalism dominates researchers across social science (Alvesson & Sandberg, 2013).

In public contexts, the incrementalist likes to say: 'more research is needed'.

'I am doing something which only few people can understand': Esotericism

In academia, there are several types of esotericism. One variant is scientific and stresses the importance of learning and knowledge in its full depth. The more extreme esotericism becomes, the more specialization it seeks, the narrower the audience it addresses, and the more abstruse the language it uses. Esotericism stresses the importance of mastering every detail of a particular theoretical tradition—for example gender theory, poststructuralism, Marxist theory, psychoanalysis, ANT (Actor–Network Theory), system theory, institutional theory—in order to understand its every text, before allowing a researcher to make his/her own contribution. As critical management scholars Cederström and Hoedemakers describe with frankness the early years at their respective business schools, this feeling of being admitted to a certain elite group can be quite elusive:

> At the start, we clung on to the belief that there surely must be something real, something hidden, behind these empty words of 'impact', 'research excellence' and 'student-led teaching'. Once we would be allowed behind the curtain, we would take up our space as fully fledged academics who knew better than the latest fads: we would be critical management scholars. Scholars, in the true sense of the word, who took up positions in business schools but wrote about power, domination, control and read Marx, Foucault and Derrida. We knew in our heart of hearts that behind the glitzy facade of the business school website with all its salesmanship, there would be a buzzing undercurrent of critical scholarship. (Cederström & Hoedemaekers, 2012, p. 232)

Esotericism frequently shows signs of elitist tendencies, when one's own group is described as being enlightened while all others are assumed to suffer from various forms of false consciousness or have not engaged sufficiently in The Theory or The Method. This has been quite a common tendency in critical studies. Thus, Martin Parker, while acknowledging that his work as journal editor was contributing to the publish-or-perish-race, claimed special privileges for his journal: 'I even wrote and co-wrote editorials in which I/we insisted that this journal was different, and that we didn't care about playing citation games', he now admits (Parker, 2013, p. 473). If the ritualist meaning stems from enforcing and observing elaborate scientific canons, the esotericist derives satisfaction from the obscure, inaccessible, and highly specialized nature of the knowledge that he/she handles. The fact that the general public and a majority of colleagues show no interest in the esotericist's research is not seen as an issue, but, on the contrary, as proof that the esotericist is doing something important. In public contexts, the esotericist likes to say: 'that's an incredibly complex question'. And: 'you really need to understand (a celebrated great thinker) to grasp this issue', often in combination with the incrementalist's motto 'more research is needed'.

'I use the right words and therefore I am good': Discursivism

Like the esotericist, the discursivist is keenly concerned with highly special-ized and frequently abstruse research but is especially sensitive to the use of language and the meaning of words. All researchers are supposed to seek to use precise language to avoid misunderstandings, but for the discursivist, correct and, above all, *advanced*, vocabulary has an intrinsic value. Certain forms of discourse are based on the esoteric rationale that everyday language is far too diverse or ideologically tainted to lead to new insights. The discursivist thus approaches the command of a particular jargon as an art form. Definitions become of the essence and his/her text is laden with underlinings, scare quotation marks, capital letters and other signs, meaningful to those in the microtribe but usually entirely meaningless to others. The fact that most people cannot understand what the discursivist is talking about, far less writing about, is as it should be. It is possible that the discursivist believes that it is up to the interpreters further down the business chain (journalists or lecturers) to pass the word on, even if in a vulgarized form, to the public and students. This is of course highly unlikely. The discursivist is rarely offered the opportunity to say something in public contexts, but when this does happen it can sound like this: 'this is where the Other's *objet petit a* interpellates as an imaginary *dénouement*'.

'I am doing something which is extremely important for me': Egocentrism

At the extreme end of the narcissistic spectrum, we meet the egocentrist researcher. He/she is concerned primarily with self-actualization which can assume forms entirely incomprehensible to others. Egocentric researchers may be entirely absorbed in a particular philosophy, art form, literary genre, idolized hero figure, method, or theory which, to them is more important than anything else, and fills their life with meaning. Unlike the esotericist, the egocentric researcher can at times create a critical distance from his/her favourite object—the important thing for the egocentric researcher is not to contribute to a particular field of knowledge as to celebrate and extol it as priceless and unique. For this reason, egocentric researchers can, paradoxically, consume books and literature with a passion. Their works are often of an exegetic type, interpreting what others *actually* meant. In rare cases, egocentric researchers can succeed in liberating themselves from existing authorities and produce original and valuable work. More frequently, however, they are liable to be alone in finding their work interesting and important, viewing themselves as solitary geniuses, whose work will be vindicated in time. When asked about their work, egocentric researchers may, similar to esotericists, claim 'My work is too complex to be understood by the wider public.'

'It may not lead to much valuable knowledge but I'm having fun': Hedonism

The hedonist matches the egocentrist's narcissism but lacks his/her belief in the seriousness of his/her work. For the hedonist, the important thing is not to make a contribution or to actualize themselves but to have fun. Hedonist researchers may be well aware that they are engaged in research and writings that are unlikely to generate any meaningful or valuable knowledge but to them this is not a problem. It is true that hedonist researchers suffer from the close scrutiny and editing rounds of academic publishing, but at the same time, they find a narcissistic pleasure in destabilizing the serious predictability of other researchers with unorthodox or witty musings on what they experience as 'fun'. Getting articles on 'The representation of professional service markets in *The Simpsons*' (Ellis, 2008), or on 'Parody subversion and the politics of gender at work: the case of Futurama's "Raging Bender"' (Pullen & Rhodes, 2013) through the rigorous review procedures of academic journals may be viewed as brilliant achievements in injecting 'fun' into an otherwise boring discipline—even if the primary point of research is not generally viewed as entertaining the researchers themselves (or their colleagues, who probably are more inclined to read even more entertaining papers than articles trying to be funny).

The competition and fantasy of getting a top journal hit may also stimulate hedonist desires. In an article on 'Journal list fetishism and the perversion of scholarship', Willmott likened the competition to 'the application of a ligature to restrict the free flow of oxygen to the brain' as a fetishized act of autoeroticism. For real 'asphyxiologists', Willmott points out, 'the fantasy object is not, of course, the top journal "hit" but, instead, the erotically charged images of a fantasy death'. If this parallel sounds far-fetched, Willmott also suggests the metaphor of the shoe to describe the journal fetishism: 'The highly ranked journal is like a shoe into which our scholarly activity is painfully, yet pleasurably, "horned" with unintended and, as I have argued, detrimental consequences for research culture and even for funding' (Willmott, 2011, p. 438).

In public, the hedonist likes to say: 'those who have had the most fun when they die are the winners'.

'My research is useless and so am I': Self-Denigration

The pressures of academic research and the continuous emphasis on excellence and originality prompts some researchers, and often highly gifted ones, to question their own abilities. Faced with repeated rejections, frustrating revisions, and constant fault-finding, nit-picking, and hair-splitting, the self-esteem of some researchers gradually evaporates to nothing, leaving a sense of barely keeping themselves afloat. Their main concern is then no longer to do meaningful research, but to address their own impostor syndrome feelings (Knights & Clarke, 2014). As an example, a thirty-four-year-old associate professor anonymously wrote to the *Guardian* about her sense of feeling guilty for not working hard enough, and of setting up targets about where to publish in order to have something to aspire to: 'If my colleagues hit these targets before I do, I feel jealous and question my abilities. Once I fulfil my objectives, I do not feel any satisfaction either' (Anonymous, 2014). The substance of the research quickly becomes secondary to the self-denigrating academic quoted above: 'We rarely contribute anything substantial to knowledge. Often we publish and re-publish the same research.' According to this person, many of her colleagues are crushed by senior professors at the beginning of their careers. As they mature, they learn how to brag about their 'achievements', but with hardly any conviction. 'They are trying to convince themselves and others that they are doing something worthy [. . .] As people grow up, they try to prove that they are now the seniors. This is the only way they can appease their own crushed egos.' Self-denigrating researchers are likely to experience themselves as walking wounded, spending a lifetime seeking to overcome their trauma, sometimes by swapping self-denigration for cynicism or careerism. Or as one lecturer says: 'I do feel quite often a sense of inadequacy . . . yeah, the old imposter syndrome' (Knights & Clarke 2014, p. 341).

In public, self-denigrating researchers find it hard to make their voices heard. They are likely to hide behind platitudes like 'This is a hard world', or rationalizations like 'People of my gender/race/political persuasion/class background, age etc. find it impossible to gain a place in the sun.'

'It may be meaningless, but look how fast I'm climbing the ladder!': Careerism

The university world, with its grades, many levels of hierarchy, and constant comparisons of merit is a veritable Eldorado for the careerist, regardless of the recurrent legitimacy crises of different disciplines. Careerist researchers, often individuals who were top in their school class and placed great value on this, may be motivated by a craving for power, status, or even revenge, but they may also have higher motives. It is not uncommon for the careerist to think that he or she only has to take *one more step* before a path-breaking line of research can begin. The careerist belief that 'I do not like what I am writing, but I have to finish it in order to move on' is likely to hit most researchers once in a while. Current work may be meaningless but it is a necessary step towards meaningful work in the future. Thus, the Norwegian sociologist Karin Widerberg confesses that she always had the sense that 'something was wrong' while writing her PhD thesis. The 'conclusions were of course predictable, they only followed from the postulates of the theory'. The formalism of her design 'killed all pleasure and creativity': 'I had to force myself into writing in a language that was not mine and in a form that was alien to me. It was all about controlling the material and the theory, *and finishing* it' (Widerberg, 2014, p. 222). Sometimes people give priority to their career just in order to reduce their anxiety about their worth and security: 'I want to feel relatively not under threat in my work, so I suppose I mean "secure". And recognized, yeah... a promotion or progression or something' (Knights & Clarke 2014, p. 343). Sometimes people are into 'a kind of sell-out a little bit because you're doing what they ask but then it gives you more freedom. But I'm happy to sell out then if that is the case' (p. 347).

Sometimes people feel that there really is no alternative. The problem arises when we find ourselves continually believing that we have to become a little more established before we can begin to do meaningful research. During their postgraduate period, many careerists come to believe that they must gain a PhD in order to have the necessary freedom; but they then discover that postdoctoral freedom is even smaller. This is the point at which the hunt for grants and lectureships begins, when everything is justified in the name of obtaining a safe and permanent job. When they finally achieve financial security, their desire shifts to promotion and then obtaining the title of professor, and by the time that this is attained, careerists have normally forgotten their old ambitions, except, maybe, as naïve youthful dreams. Skills and habits are strongly geared to an instrumental, opportunistic logic.

As another anonymous researcher explained in the *Guardian*, he agreed to list his professor as an author on many of his papers although the professor had not contributed to them: 'My professor is in a position of power, and refusing to do so could limit my own career opportunities. He could refuse to assign any master's students to my projects, meaning I have less manpower or refuse to nominate me for prizes' (Anonymous, 2015a). Clearly there is a power relation here, but not receiving master's students as manpower or losing the opportunity of being nominated for prizes might be a price worth paying for autonomy and integrity. Power does not necessarily imply subordination, but for some careerists, symbolic rewards are more important than autonomy.

In public, the careerist may say: 'I need to be really established and have a top standing in the field before I can do bold, risky and significant work.'

'While doing like everyone else, I choose to suffer heroically': Radical Despair

There are some researchers who, like hedonists, are aware of being engaged in meaningless research, but, unlike hedonists, are unable to transform it into 'fun'. These researchers are prone to complain about the state of the academy and in particular about 'the pressure to publish'. Towards the evening, when some alcohol has been consumed and 'speaking freely' is allowed, a real battle to outshine others, with different expressions of despair, may break out. Here, we see an extreme version of what Georg Lukács called the 'Grand Hotel *Abgrund*' (Jay, 1973, p. 309) in which critical scholars often enjoy relatively comfortable lives, but prefer emphasizing power structures and institutional obstacles as an excuse for not engaging in an active transformation of the system. Overt expressions of radical despair, accompanied by strident criticisms of 'the system', of its management, and of all attempts to reform it, often serve as confirmations of these academics' radical credentials. In the UK, REF blaming is a popular activity, constructing a world where one is a victim of the world's injustices, preventing oneself from doing the really interesting and vital research a fair world would make possible. Radical despair may prompt some of these researchers to lapse into total cynicism, into clinical depression, or may lead them to abandon academia altogether.

A typical experience would be something like this one: 'I am in the business to help my department to get a higher score in the RAE and the only way I can do this is by doing more and more arcane stuff' (Knights & Clarke 2014, p. 345). In public contexts, the despairing researchers are sometimes heard to say: 'The system is corrupt to the core, nothing can be done to change it, so we might as well grin and bear it.'

On 'Better' Motives

The positive—or even perhaps the nuanced—person may now feel that we are unfair and one-sided and only point at the 'dark' side of academics' motivations. Needless to say, there are also other orientations and motives, well summarized by Habermas' (1972) three knowledge interests: technical control for problem-solving, increasing human understanding, and emancipation from social domination. Probably the majority of all academics at least occasionally feel engaged in what they do, because they find the topics and research interesting, and they hope or are convinced that they have something important to say. We ourselves feel like that for at least part, or even most, of the time. (But this may be a delusion—it is very easy to fall victim to wishful thinking and a self-serving bias.)

We find it more important to draw attention to the motives and rationales that are central behind the sad state of affairs of social science. Initial 'good' motives often seem to be weakened and the rationales which we identified in this chapter become more salient when the great contribution to mankind (or even a specific audience) is not really produced as intended, and the pressure to get published feels urgent. When researchers feel convinced they have, or work intensively, to develop a good idea, are willing to make an effort to do an innovative and imaginative study, and devote much attention to producing texts that are inviting and create positive experiences, all is fine—at least if these feelings are confirmed. Central motives are then: intellectual curiosity, open-mindedness, willingness to reflect and challenge one's own and microtribes' assumptions and vocabulary, to take risks, to make 'non-convenient' empirical work, to devote much time to interpretation and writing, and possibly postpone finishing the PhD or a promotion until one has something important to say.

We are not denying that these motives are part of many academics' research efforts and occasionally there are outcomes in line with these initial motives. Our ambition is to point out that these seem to be increasingly marginal, and encourage a different balance between 'positive' and 'negative' personal drivers and rationales for researchers.

In Conclusion

All of the above rationales provide researchers with justifications for making sense of spending much of their lives engaged in meaningless research, seeking solace in their membership of various microtribes of like-minded individuals, wrapped up in their cocoons of isolation and irrelevance. It is for this reason that individual academics can readily swap one rationale for another, slipping easily from ritualism to careerism to egocentrism and so forth. The net result is research outputs that can stand as objects of envy, as objects of pride, as objects of pity and despair, as objects of ridicule and derision, and even as objects of love, but ultimately objects devoid of social or political meaning.

The rationales are not mutually exclusive, and the same person can drift between them all from day to day. They may also be guided by other more worthwhile drivers from the broader academic community and society, including a love for their discipline and work, a deep desire to defend a cause, or even to change society. As said above, this set of rationales is not meant to be exhaustive. Uncertainty about the 'real' drivers is notorious, we cannot directly access people's motives (Martin, 2011; Mills, 1940) and there is a discrepancy between espoused rationales and those in action. Deeply buried unconscious motives, such as to outcompete a more successful sibling, to impress a long dead parent, or to compensate for an early life trauma, can also exercise an influence. Researchers, like other people, are liable to rationalize their ambitions. The complexities and variations around rationales as well as outcomes need to be recognized. Of course, hedonism, egocentrism, careerism, and so on do not preclude valuable knowledge outcomes just as highly moral motives do not prevent researchers from producing work of doubtful value and relevance. Yet, these rationales offer researchers ready-made excuses and rationalizations for writing articles or monographs that they themselves recognize—or should recognize—as having limited meaning and value.

Does the analysis of rationales like these entail an individualization of the problems academics are facing? Not necessarily. Nor do we think that these rationales impose any insuperable obstacles to the effort of recovering meaning for social science research. On the contrary, the malaise expressed by most of these rationales and the wider malaise and discontent regarding research assessment systems and the organization of the university (Willmott, 2011) make this effort particularly promising. Instead of seeking excuses and rationalizations for producing work of limited interest and even more limited social relevance, our ambition is to examine how meaning may resume its rightful place in social science discourses—and how the work of academics may cease being purely of 'academic interest'.

5

Methodologies and Writings that Turn into Black Holes of Meaning

The claim that social science is in crisis is not new. In the field of sociology, crises have been declared ever since the 1930s. Fragmentation, endless repetition of old ideas, poor methods and, above all, a lack of general relevance are recurring themes in the crisis literature (for example, Gouldner, 1970; Lynd, 1939). The best-known example is C. Wright Mills' criticism of sociology in *The Sociological Imagination*.

Mills identified two tendencies which he claimed were destroying social science. The first tendency was the fascination with, and the gravity of, Grand Theory, that is, a system construction aiming to explain 'everything' with a 'confused verbiage' (Mills, 2000 [1959], p. 27). The other tendency was the 'Abstracted Empiricism', in which sociologists became method focussed and learned certain techniques to run data with which they could easily lend themselves to instrumental interests outside academia (Mills, 2000 [1959], p. 50). In both of these tendencies, *jargon* was an essential tool to create the impression of 'science'. Mills' 'translations' of the functionalist Talcott Parsons' indigestible prose remains among the most entertaining reading found in social science. By translating Parsons' jargon-heavy prose into readable English, Mills demonstrated how much sociology consists of a fragile skeleton of mundane insights wrapped in thick layers of advanced linguistic clothing. The shameless speculations and empty distinctions do not enlarge our understanding, according to Mills. They are tools used to create legitimacy and gain the reader's acceptance by means of confusion and exhaustion. It would simply take too much time and work to demonstrate the very limited value of such theory.

Since Mills, many have bemoaned what van Maanen calls 'the impersonal, formulaic and dull discourse so loved by journal editors'. According to van Maanen, scholarly discourse has become 'impoverished, stiff, sanitized and humorless' (1995, p. 687). Another adjective coined by Perrow (1986, p. 176) is 'asphalted'. This discourse not only alienates readers, but, as Tourish and

Willmott (2015, p. 43) put it, is 'also soul destroying for its authors to write'. And the readers, who like Richardson (2000, p. 924) often are forced to read, have little option but to yawn 'through numerous supposedly exemplary qualitative studies', 'half read, half scanned'.

Almost fifty years after Mills' critique, Burawoy attempted to breathe new life into the debate and offer a concrete alternative by launching the concept of *public sociology*. Burawoy's basic argument is that social science has become professionalized, which has led to it becoming isolated and, ironically, less relevant to the society around it. In certain disciplines, notably economics, psychology, and sociology, a driver in the move towards professionalization has been a 'science complex' in which natural science provides the model of how all scientific inquiry should be pursued. As a consequence, the emphasis on methods has increased hugely since Mills' critique while tolerance for Grand Theory has declined (see also Swedberg, 2012). Many empirical studies, in themselves trivial, do of course seek to 'boost' their theoretical claims by attaching themselves to theories, such as 'transactional cost economics', 'post-colonialism', 'institutional theory', or 'discourse', even though their contribution to these theories is minimal.

Professionalization eliminates the problem of whether those outside the profession understand or find any interest in its 'discoveries'. The research community lives its own life. Public sociology on the other side reaches outwards, but unlike its more instrumentalist twin *policy sociology*, it is intended first and foremost for the general public, at the same time as it aims to say something new and meaningful based on research. Sociology's 'promise' as expressed by Mills (2000 [1959], p. 130)—helping people understand that some of the problems we experience as personal troubles are in fact public issues—is mentioned explicitly by Burawoy. Such an outward-reaching social science is also reflexive in the sense that it is concerned with its ability to act as a transformative power. Its ambition is to say something new and meaningful and to achieve a wider acceptance for it. Its underlying rationale is that the object of social science—society—is not static, and it comprises the various theories and ideas *about* society. The various understandings and theories of the problems faced by society are themselves constitutive of society. If improving our understanding is to be more than a matter of the preferential right of interpretation, considerable demands must be made on 'presenting research findings in an accessible manner for a lay audience' (Burawoy, 2005, p. 12). In an attempt to counter the anxiety of contact with broader groups, Burawoy started *Contexts*, a referee-reviewed journal for public sociology. The idea was that *Contexts* would become a channel which would take social science to the general public. Since its launch in 2002, many, including Burawoy, have agreed that the attempt was unsuccessful. *Contexts* has a substantial readership, but is made up almost exclusively of researchers.

One factor Burawoy has not taken into account is how much popularization sociology really deserves. Although the agenda has changed somewhat since public sociology was first launched, Burawoy is first and foremost interested in changing the form and forum of the writing. He implicitly assumes that there is important substance in social science which is being withheld from the general public. But is this true? Already in 1985, sociologist Patricia Wilner provided an inventory of all the articles published between 1936 and 1982 in the *American Sociological Review*, revealing that the journal had largely neglected the main social issues in the public debate during its first forty-six years. According to her calculations, between 1936 and 1941, only 6.4 per cent of the articles addressed questions relating to the Great Depression. Likewise, between 1947 and 1956 around 1 per cent of the articles dealt with McCarthyism and the Cold War (Wilner, 1985). Sociology lacking social relevance is, in other words, not a new phenomenon, and in all likelihood is something all professional sociologists have experienced personally.

As we have already argued, we believe that social science at large is not only facing a problem of *style* but also of *substance*. Formulaic papers are not only the consequence of bad writing, but of the entire research process and more broadly of formulaic mindsets. In this chapter, we discuss the academic norms and methods that tend to produce well-referenced and 'appropriate' publications with very little to say. What we see is a streamlined way of thinking about research that eliminates chances of imagination, serendipity, and accidental discovery that are crucial to scientific progress. We concentrate our analysis on four aspects of this streamlining. First, there is an overall instrumentalization of academic research that is institutionally related to the reward structures that we have already analysed. Second, the conventional method of guaranteeing 'return on investment' is to address 'gaps' in the literature rather than complex problems. Third, to fill these gaps in a passably 'scientific' manner, researchers resort to various forms of empiricism that have been approved within their respective microtribes. Fourth, to pacify reviewers, gain recognition within one's microtribe, and appear cultivated (or 'precise' as most would say), researchers learn to develop jargon-packed and obscure styles of writing. These styles of writing do not necessarily hide any meaningful content from the readers. As Billig puts it, the tendency is rather to use 'an impressive concept, not to identify a discovery, but to cover a lack of discovery' (Billig, 2013, p. 51).

Specialization and the Triumph of Technique over Meaning

Intense instrumentalism, the drive to promote career and promotion chances, is as we noted earlier, a key factor behind the depletion of meaning in social science research. This is not a new phenomenon in academic life, as our references to Mills' complaints testify, but its extent and its nakedness are unprecedented.

> In general I see very few people doing work they think important for anything but the tenure and promotion treadmill. This seems less a matter of personal or professional choice than the way our professionalization project clamped down on our sense of purpose. (Senior academic, personal correspondence)

Instrumentalism is inculcated in young researchers in regular workshops on 'publishing high-impact research'—'high impact' as defined as publishing in US A-journals. If one were to track where the methodological problems begin in each individual research process, this is where to look. Not only does instrumentalism of this kind bracket the striving for meaning from the outset, it also has very concrete effects on how research projects are conducted.

In a workshop in which one of us participated, one presenter started by asking 'How can we be sure to get "a high return on investment" in our research projects?' Such extreme instrumentalism can be labelled roisearch (ROI-search), a far cry from curiosity-driven, uncertainty-acknowledging studies where the end point of discovery cannot be guaranteed in advance (Alvesson 2013b). The transition *from research to roisearch* marks a deep change of the academic mindset, one in which naked careerism reigns supreme, reflecting a general trend towards a narcissism that craves external validation and seeks ever more glamorous and superficial signs to this end. Insecurity about self-worth becomes pervasive, and seeks to reassure itself by checking citations counts and comparing 'starred publications' to those of other researchers. A hyper-sensitivity about status, identity, and self-esteem make narcissism rampant.

In some respects, this hyper-sensitivity about identity and craving for external recognition can be seen as a part of a general contemporary trend for *motivation to act as a surrogate for meaning.* Sievers (1986, p.335) suggests that the contemporary working life has turned to motivation to make up 'for the meaning of work and life which is increasingly lost through the high frequency of fragmentation and splitting in our contemporary work enterprises'. Such fragmentation and splitting have reached unprecedented proportions in our times when most researchers can at best be heard in tiny forums that we termed research microtribes. Belonging to such a microtribe (and occasionally to more than one) is vital for today's researcher. Without such a microtribe, today's researcher is out in the wilderness. He or she wanders around conferences lost and ignored by others, who talk animatedly to each other building networks and making plans; his or her paper submissions hit wall after wall or rejection on grounds of not being rooted in existing literature and meeting the mindset of a selected microtribe audience. Such a researcher has no way of making his or her voice heard; they are reduced to being a non-researcher no matter what work they are doing.

The importance of the research microtribe was appreciated by Mills in referring to them as 'cliques' whose function it is to regulate and set the terms of academic competition. Belonging to a clique meant, according to Mills, enjoying and reproducing: 'the giving of friendly advice to younger men; job offers and recommendations of promotion; the assignment of books to admiring reviewers; the ready acceptance of articles and books for publication; the allocation of research funds; arranging or politicking for honorific positions within professional associations and on editorial boards of professional journals' (Mills, 2000 [1959], p. 107).

Becoming part of a research microtribe requires, almost invariably, investing in a narrow subfield. This may require great pains in terms of reading, networking, and developing a self-imposed myopia focussing on a limited set of questions which for most people are meaningless, or at best, incomprehensible. Once inside the microtribe, researchers (roisearchers) are normally reluctant to leave, at least before they have had a strong return on their investment. Thus, they continuously scrutinize publications in the microtribes' subfield, learning its conventions and fashions, cultivating the right connections. They learn how to satisfy the demands of the other subspecialists assessing papers and being crucial for careers. As time goes by, venturing beyond this habitat becomes risky. Even seasoned researchers who feel that they have a contribution to make in a different microtribe from the one with which they are usually identified risk rejection and dismissal due to their ostensible ignorance of its conventions and assumptions. This is why we so often hear researchers responding to journalists' queries with the seemingly prudent 'I'm afraid it's outside my field of research.' Many of them simply do not know anything else.

Specialization and fragmentation of scholarship have reached unprecedented heights with the rise of mass education. From the early academics who, as late as the nineteenth century, taught and did research in several disciplines such as philosophy, mathematics, and chemistry, we have created academics who cannot master even a single discipline, but only small subfields. This fragmentation is technologically accelerated by the increasing division of labour, including academic journals which were once read in their entirety but are now hardly more than databases for electronic browsing and citation-fishing. This enables researchers to follow exclusively the publications of members of their microtribe without the risk of wasting their time on other material. Today, what Mills called 'the technician' applies not only to the quantitative social science that he associated with 'abstracted empiricism'. Rather depressingly, we now witness the same phenomenon in qualitative studies with their increasing emphasis on the precision and rigour of coding routines and the standardization of what counts as adequate empirical material on which to theorize. The problem is that this is very seldom guided by, or leads to, a new idea or the reporting of rich data. An established framework broadly confirmed by the data leads to 'predictable' findings.

Specialization as well as concept fetishism have now become as endemic in qualitative studies as they were in quantitative ones. Researchers will typically focus on a particular concept or variable (not least gender, ethnicity, identity, age, sexuality, leadership, profession, career, knowledge management, and so on) and then demonstrate its importance in study after study in different contexts. Generally these studies confirm the convictions and commitments of the researcher. Foucauldians, poststructuralists, institutional theorists, discourse analysts, feminists, and others typically prove that they were right from the beginning. In this way, hundreds of studies of 'doing gender' (interactions and acts where actors demonstrate compliance with norms of gender appropriate behaviour) have been conducted, typically using the framework of West and Zimmerman (1987) and unsurprisingly they all confirm that people are busy 'doing gender' (Deutsch, 2007).

The proliferation of research microtribes and the vigilance with which they patrol their membership and boundaries induces a myopic conformity which allows little room for independent and critical thinking, for any cross-fertilization with concepts and theories from other fields, or for a concern for the social value and meaning of the microtribe's 'contribution'. Instead, we see an increasing concern for 'contributing' *to the microtribe*, confirming the research box the tribe tends to move within.

Gap-Spotting

The dominance of microtribal conventions and the rigour with which they seek to enforce them has now made it virtually impossible to present a new theory questioning established truths in the field in the 8,000 words of the standard journal article. This was not always so. Mills' (1940) brilliant piece on motives was only ten pages. Major contributions even after Mills' criticisms could still be made in relatively short articles. Take, for instance, Sykes and Matza's foundational text on delinquency (1957) expounded in a mere six pages of text, as was Bachrach and Baratz' (1962) influential article on agenda-setting as a key element of power, Sievers' (1986) seminal reflections on motivation and meaning noted earlier in a mere fifteen pages, Scott and Lyman's (1968) pivotal text of accounts in sixteen pages, and even Dimaggio and Powell's (1983) hugely cited work on institutional isomorphism in thirteen pages. All of these texts would stand a chance of being published today, when many published articles have bloated to 15,000 or even 20,000 words and frequently over 200 cited references. Having at least one reference after each sentence (or preferably three) has become a sign of good scholarship, signalling that one has read a lot and that each argument and finding is firmly rooted in earlier research. To be able to produce this type of text, to learn what is fashionable within a microtribe, is of the essence. Once you have found your way into the microtribe, however, you must learn to produce 'contributions'.

The standard response of researchers to this situation has been to seek to identify a gap in a microtribes' literature and then claim that their contribution is to fill the gap. Gap-spotting becomes the dominant spark for a research paper (Alvesson & Sandberg, 2013). No matter how tiny the gap, no matter how irrelevant it is, and even if it is only a rhetorical device to persuade fellow tribe members, the gap in the literature is now key. Articles based on gap-spotting are generally motivated by arguments such as: 'no previous study has specifically examined the link between x and y' or 'the relation between x and y in the context of z'. X and y can then represent various phenomena such as 'military dictators' and 'military interventions in politics' (Svolik, 2013), or 'friendship and peer acceptance at school' and 'early adolescents' adjustment across the middle school transition' (Kingery, Erdley, & Marshall, 2011) or 'the availability of tobacco products' and 'socioeconomic and racial/ethic characteristics of neighbourhoods' (Siahpush, Jones, Singh, Timsina, & Martin, 2010).

A survey of a number of research articles in education, management, psychology, and sociology indicated that the majority of them subscribed to the gap-spotting approach (Alvesson & Sandberg, 2013). This results in incremental work, adding marginally, if at all, to existing knowledge. Its ambition is never to chart a new territory of knowledge or to challenge tacit assumptions or indeed to contribute something meaningful and relevant to society. Gap-spotting can occasionally lead to original results but its main concern is for safety and guaranteed return on investment. By targeting what no one else is meant to have previously studied (even if there are good reasons for this neglect), researchers build on an established theory and simply aim to 'add' to this. Adding to the microtribe's literature rather than illuminating a social phenomenon in an original and insightful way is a safe way of not offending anyone. The career strategist thus avoids the risk of treading on sensitive toes.

In conclusion, we see gap-spotting as representing more than voluntary myopia. It is a method of neutralizing one's research while also guaranteeing that it lives up to standards of moderate 'novelty' and 'contribution'. It typically leads to the accumulation of similar-looking studies that seldom offer something significant.

Formulaic Empiricism

Whether quantitative or qualitative, a key ingredient in any paper in social science is to signal ultra-rationalism and a complete lack of ambiguity in the 'data collection'. The emphasis on transparency and rationality is often combined with deep mysticism. Method sections, particularly in PhD theses, often resort to grandiose statements about ontology and epistemology, inflating a modest number of interviews into 'ethnographies', or routine textual analysis into 'discourse analysis'. Authors of qualitative studies are routinely asked to respond to demands like the following:

> Clearly some detailed study of the [field] has been carried out and some interesting and conflicting narratives are presented. There is potentially rich material here. However, it is not clear how this material has been analyzed. Was some type of content analysis used? How was the material coded?   (Review of journal submission)

In order to tackle such objections, researchers learn to worry about their 'data management' and develop various formulaic coding procedures that decontextualize the empirical material in order to make it appear more objective and homogeneous than it really is. Imaginative, ad hoc, serendipity-driven studies that relied on material collected or observed opportunistically have few ways of meeting the requests for rigour, without in fact pretending to have followed a carefully constructed methodology (Gabriel, 2013). Over several rounds of revisions, such studies are liable either to rejection or to reduction to the dull, formulaic shape of the others.

Although various forms of data management may be accepted by different microtribes, social science still suffers from a lack of credibility in the eyes of the public. For a long time, social scientists have attempted to counteract this suspiciousness by seeking to emulate natural scientists; by conducting experiments, producing quantitative data and formulas to prove their point. But what is sometimes referred to as 'physics envy' tends to reduce relevance more than to increase respectability. There are exceptions, in those works that are both 'scientific' and socially relevant, such as the work of psychologists like Milgram and Kahneman, economists like Piketty (2014), sociologists like Townsend (1979), and epidemiologists like Wilkinson and Pickett (2010). Many interesting and socially relevant ideas reach a wider public when they are well-written with no special effort to prove their scientific credentials (good examples include Fromm, 1941, 1976; Riesman et al., 1950; Linder, 1969; Sennett, 1998). However, in the quest for finding publishable 'significant results'—what often boils down to chasing p-values below 0.05—statistical significance only rarely implies significantly meaningful results.

In recent years, an even more disturbing problem of quantitative methods within social science has been brought to light. What is supposed to be the most 'rigorous' of methods—experiments—may not be very rigorous at all.

As every textbook on philosophy of science or method will tell you, a fundamental condition for reliability in experiment studies is that of reproducibility—that a certain study or experiment can be duplicated. Yet how much have the same scientists who teach students the virtue of reproducibility actually been involved in replicating studies?

In the early 2010s a turn towards humility could be noticed among some natural scientists. This was particularly noticeable in cell biology when two industrial laboratories replicated a large number of landmark studies and found that the original results could only be reproduced in 11 per cent and 25 per cent of cases respectively (Begley & Ellis, 2012).

The most ambitious and systematic reproducibility study conducted was published three years later, in 2015, but in this study the focus was set on social science, or more specifically one hundred psychological experiments published in three top-ranked journals: *Psychological Science, Journal of Personality and Social Psychology,* and *Learning, Memory, and Cognition.* The study required the collaboration of 270 psychologists—the Open Science Collaboration—who in the Introduction to their article stated: 'Scientific claims should not gain credence because of the status or authority of their originator but by the replicability of their supporting evidence' (OSC, 2015, p. 943). But while 97 per cent of the one hundred studies originally reported statistically significant results, only 36 per cent of the replications did. Hence, the credence was by the stated standard unsubstantiated. The Federal Reserve economists Chang and Li also set about researching how many of the results published in top economic journals could be replicated. Of sixty-seven papers, only one-third of the results could be independently replicated without the help of the original authors. With their help, 49 per cent could. Chang and Li contended that 'because we are able to replicate less than half of the papers in our sample, we assert that economics research is usually not replicable' (Chang & Li, 2015, p. 11). Subsequently, Camerer et al. (2016) attempted to repeat eighteen studies in leading economic journals. The result that 61 per cent could be replicated successfully was later described by Camerer as 'pretty encouraging' (Basken, 2016). This positive interpretation of the rather poor results was most likely due to the low reproducibility rate of the earlier studies.

One can here add that the use of experiments in social science typically means the study of students in simplified and artificial settings, which are less difficult to replicate than, for example, more complex case studies or interview- based research.[1] The ideal of replicability is therefore less of a concern for

---

[1] There are for sure many areas where the evidence seems to point in the same direction, for example, that a high level of public administration/low level of corruption is crucial for

observation studies, but even if the aim of social science were to discern behavioural patterns or laws that transcend cultural and historical circumstances—an aim many would dispute—there would be no guarantee that resorting to statistics and experiments would work. As Ioannidis suggests in his classic essay 'Why most published research findings are false', the hotter a scientific field becomes with different microtribes competing against each other, the less likely the research findings are to be true:

> Each team may prioritize on pursuing and disseminating its most impressive 'positive' results. 'Negative' results may become attractive for dissemination only if some other team has found a 'positive' association on the same question. In that case, it may be attractive to refute a claim made in some prestigious journal.
>
> (Ioannidis, 2005, p. 698)

In other words, within the institutional constraints of modern academia there is a variety of contingencies, social pressures, and endeavours that may compromise any methodology no matter how rigorous and solid its theoretical foundation is. This does not legitimize relativism or disregard for careful empirical studies, yet it might call for a shift in focus to what the sociologist Richard Swedberg calls 'theorizing'. Swedberg argues that the 'context of discovery', in which theorizing takes place, has been deliberately undertheorized from Popper and onwards. This is why he embarks on discerning different stages of the theorizing process: from the subtle and often subconscious practices of introspection and observation to the more formal stages of naming, conceptualizing, and guessing at explanations (Swedberg, 2012). Unlike the methodological testing of theories (taking place in the 'context of justification'), theorizing is, in Swedberg's words, 'deeply democratic' since there are no institutional or economic barriers surrounding it, and since everyone is capable of doing it. Quoting Coleridge, Swedberg suggests that 'to think at all is to theorize' (Swedberg, 2012, p. 29). However, while the development of methods has become the primary focus within sociology during the last fifty years, theory development has stood relatively still. Whether this has led to any real amelioration of sociological methods is today an open question.

---

citizen well-being and matters much more than the level of democracy, which seems to be almost irrelevant in this respect (Rothstein, 2015). Often a large number of questionnaires superficially showing convergence only really demonstrate that subjects tend to fill in X's in questionnaires in similar ways and express tautology, for example, that 'transformational leadership' (based on inspiration and consideration) leads to a variety of 'good' effects (Van Knippenberg & Sitkin, 2013). Qualitative research based on the idea that people 'do gender', regularly confirms and reproduces this assumption (Deutsch, 2007). Such research merely reflects a political and theoretical commitment to the assumption as 'truth' rather than adding any substantive empirical evidence that supports it.

Socspeak

While formulaic empiricism tends to be followed by formulaic writing, the problem of unappealing texts goes much wider than that. Increasingly, social science is guided by the desire to get published in journals, and this governs writing in sometimes absurd ways. The attempt to forestall or placate critical reviewers can easily be detected in how many articles are written. Researchers are so dependent on reviewers, that publications typically are cautious and mainstream. Published papers tend to be stripped of much originality even before the rounds of revision begin. After the revisions, there is further work with pleasing reviewers. At that point, papers often have references or sections that never would have been there if it were not for the request of certain reviewers. An apparent homogenization of content is visible, the structure has been standardized, and there is seldom any style (other than the formulaic) to speak of.

This is how academics learn to write badly. The lack of personal style, irony, and wit are clearly related to the bleak endeavour so that not even the most humourless person should be able to write a question mark in the margin.

What Mills called 'socspeak', still serves the old purpose of saying: 'I know something that is so difficult you can understand it only if you first learn my difficult language. In the meantime, you are merely a journalist, a layman, or some other sort of underdeveloped type' (Mills, 2000 [1959], p. 220).

As Mills convincingly demonstrated, much of the prose sociologists use can easily be translated to readable English. An interesting effect of such translations is that the text may lose its intellectual nimbus and reveal extreme forms of banality. Instead of repeating the examples provided by Mills, let us have a look at two contemporary examples from two relatively high-ranked journals in organization studies.

Original Text

Despite criticism of Burawoy's analysis, particularly his one-sided functionalist approach, his lack of dialectics and the assumption that consent is only created in the labour process irrespective of external relations (e.g. Clawson & Fantasia, 1983; Edwards, 1986; Gartman, 1983; Roscigno & Hodson, 2004; Thompson, 1983), similar analyses have more recently reappeared in critical workplace studies with regard to both time appropriation (Baxter & Kroll-Smith, 2005; Ladner, 2009; Maier, 2006; Townsend, 2004) and to organizational misbehavior in general (see Contu, 2008; Fleming & Spicer, 2008; Fleming, 2009; Mumby, 2005; Sewell, 2008).

Translation

> Some people criticized Burawoy for one-sidedly focusing on the labour process when explaining why workers consent, but lately others have returned to some of his ideas. Also, I have gathered lots of references and therefore I am scientific.

In this translation, we must admit, we are less indulgent towards the original author than Mills was towards Parsons. To be fair, there may be other reasons for employing a long series of references than claiming scientific authority. Authors might want to prove that they have read a lot, that they are educated, or perhaps that they know how to handle citation software such as Endnote. Be as it may, this style of writing is relatively new and we see no reason why it should be tolerated.

Original Text

> This allowed for an open enquiry into ego-dystonic compliance. By *compliance* I here mean the 'instrumental involvement for specific, extrinsic rewards' (O'Reilly & Chatman, 1986, p. 493) where the most important reward in this case was to retain a full-time job and all the economic benefits that come with it. This compliance was *ego-dystonic* in the sense that it, unlike other instances of 'willing compliance' (Barker, 1993, p. 412), was dissonant from the goals and values that the employees wanted to pursue in their jobs.

Translation

> I use a difficult word, 'ego-dystonic compliance', instead of a simple word, such as 'obedience' or 'submission'.

This translation may appear even more unjust, but since one of us has written both the original texts and the translations (Paulsen, 2015, p. 354, 2017, p. 190), we feel we have some knowledge of what the author wanted to say here. In the first version of the article, Paulsen actually did use the word 'obedience', and he also offered a stipulative definition of the concept not to confuse it with how others have used it. Unfortunately, this was not enough to please one of the reviewers who wrote a full page on the many definitions of 'obedience'. Therefore, the term 'ego-dystonic compliance' was invented. Whether the reviewer actually approved of this neologism or just gave up, we do not know. In any case, this is a clear example of how obscure language can be of help in the publication chase.

Other Examples

Needless to say, examples like these exist in abundance. A similar style can for instance be found in Clarke and Knights (2015) who 'see careerism as the preoccupation with establishing an (unattainable) secure identity that tends to deflect or render opaque any sense of a nascent ethical and embodied engagement that would be a response to ambiguity and tension around new managerialism'. This basically means that they see concerns with career as an effort to secure identity in the light of 'managerialism' at the expense of ethical considerations.

A hospital study by Currie and Spyridonidis (2016, p. 93), referring to institutional theory, claims to 'show evidence of mutual adjustment between interdependent actors in the face of institutional complexity. Aligned with Jarzabkowski et al., we detail the process of mutual adjustment—powerful agents (doctors and executive managers) enable agency for relatively less powerful agents (CHF nurse consultants), by transferring a degree of power to them. At the same time, the less powerful actors are cognizant of, and take care to align with, the logic held by their powerful counterparts, deploying strategies to minimize local conflicts in order to enchance their power'. In more straightforward language this means: the researchers have found, as others have, that the powerful give some support to the less powerful and the latter try to adjust and be cooperative and avoid conflicts.

Another off-putting writing style is to narrow the target group through referring to internal debates and writings that the reader is supposed to know in detail in order to follow the text, thereby excluding an audience that may be well read, but that has not recently studied exactly the same material as the small microtribe being specialized in a specific microtribal concern. One example is an article that starts by saying 'with their recent publication, *Reflexive Modernization*, Ulrich Beck, Anthony Giddens and Scott Lash give sufficient contours to allow one to identify some of the key theoretical problems raised by the debate. One striking and currently topical problem is highlighted by Lash's contribution which not only interestingly refracts the debate but also sharply yet quite inadvertently focuses it' (Strydom 1999, p. 45). The paper continues in the same way and it takes some time before the reader starts to get any sense of the subject matter of the debate and the key points of those involved. It is not (only) the dense vocabulary or pretentious formulations, but the use of references/name-dropping and the precondition that the reader is familiar with exactly the same writings as the author (and his mates) that excludes the reader coming from outside the microtribe. Here, we find plenty of examples of the discursivism, esotericism, and egocentrism as described in Chapter 4.

Yet, few social scientists would explain their obscure writing with the need to 'get published' or demonstrate their belonging to a specific microtribe. The traditional excuse is rather that the research they want to present is so revolutionary there are no available words to describe it, or that only people with exactly the right pre-understanding can be approached without trivializing matters. The critically disposed have their own way of saying things. The very old argument, that ordinary language is ideological and should therefore be avoided, is thus put forward by Bourdieu, among many others:

The need to resort to an *artificial language* is perhaps more compelling for sociology than for any other science. In order to break with the social philosophy that runs through everyday words and also in order to express things that ordinary language cannot express (for example, everything that lies at the level of it-goes-without-saying), the sociologist has to resort to invented words which are thereby protected, relatively at least, from the naïve projections of common sense (Bourdieu, 1993, p. 21).

No one has better questioned this line of reasoning than Billig in *Learn to Write Badly*. Most fundamentally, he points out that Bourdieu and other critics of 'ordinary language' seem to be considering 'language to be a thing, an object, possessing definite characteristics and expressing certain views. Significantly, Bourdieu talks about "ordinary language", not ordinary speakers' (Billig, 2013, p. 91). What is the 'social philosophy' inherent in 'everyday words'? And how can the very quote above—where he describes something far from an 'ordinary idea'—lack the 'artificial language' Bourdieu is otherwise very capable of using?

The jargon of socspeak is in itself worth an entire chapter and whether or not one should apply 'ordinary' or 'artificial' language when writing cannot be given any general answer—sometimes ordinary language might actually lack the nuances needed to discern a certain phenomenon. Sometimes not. However, in Billig's account, it is still possible to recognize three proliferating traps that should generally be avoided as far as possible.

First, writing with a *passive voice*—'it is argued that . . .' rather than 'I argue that . . .'—has the benefit of sounding impersonal and therefore 'scientific'. This can be especially useful when scientists write their methods sections. As Billig contends, the passive voice obscures who is the active agent. Being somewhat tedious in the long run, it is also likely to alienate the reader.

Second, another way to avoid saying who did it, is *to nominalize verbs* through different 'izations'. The extent to which researchers nominalize is perhaps most visible in how discourse analysts who are critical of this linguistic practice prefer the word 'nominalization' (instead of 'to nominalize'). The same discourse analysts usually prefer to talk about how 'power operates' rather than how people who have power use their power in different ways. Again, the agents (or to use a nominalization, 'agency') disappear from the analysis.

Third, in the interest of sounding innovative, scientists may also fall back on *grandiose nominalizations*. Here, Billig takes two interesting examples. 'Governmentality' (and its processual variant 'governmentalization') is a typical nominalization that, although very imprecise, has had a huge success in attracting the interest of other researchers. In the debates on the concept of governmentality that followed Rose and Miller's (2010) article in the *British Journal of Sociology*, the confusion caused by the concept's reifying character has been so deep that it is sometimes hard to know whether researchers use it to describe 'governmentality' as a field of study, or as a type of government. Another example of grandiose nominalizing, is how 'analysing texts and interviewing their authors' can be conceptualized into a methodology called 'phenomenography' (Marton, 1986), growing into a 'research field' of its own. 'Try Phenomenography right away'—Billig mocks the grandiosity—'Improve your research with new scientifically tested Phenomenography' (Billig, 2013, p. 53).

Other good examples are all the work on 'discourse', 'institution', and 'leadership'. Almost everything trivial can be blown up and made into something significant and impressive through simply framing it with the use of a grandiose but often deceptive and meaningless label. This is not to say that all or even the large majority of all work using these labels fails to contribute to good knowledge. But the overall problem of boosting trivial work and contributions with high-flying labels and pretences to contribute to Big Theory is huge, and contributes to the massive expansion of publications that may look impressive for the uncritical eye, but have very little to say to people who have not bought into the love for the specific version of socspeak that unites the microtribe.

In Conclusion

As we have demonstrated in this chapter, socspeak is but the tip of an iceberg, consisting of a long range of choices that have to do with the formulation of research questions, ambitions to maximize one's 'output', looking for 'gaps' in the literature that will excuse myopic scopes, and resorting to 'methods' accepted by the microtribe that may turn out to be flawed, producing irreproducible results. An efficient way of covering up for these fundamental weaknesses is to obscure them with a language that is so dreadful that only a handful of people will be able to read through the texts. Again, making one's research irrelevant for the general public is to a large extent a self-imposed effort.

Part II
Recovery of Meaning

6

Recovering Meaning by Reforming Academic Identities and Practices

In Part I of this book, we argued that there is a proliferation of meaningless social research of no value to society and academia and dubious value to most authors. We noted the widespread dissatisfaction with what has become a publishing 'game', the grip that this game exercises in the practices of academics and academic institutions including university departments and academic journals, their publishers and editors, and analysed some of the mechanisms that sustain and enhance this grip at individual and institutional levels.

Part II offers a number of proposals and suggestions for recovering meaning in social science research at individual, institutional, and policy levels. We believe that these measures offer the prospect of many small 'wins' through which the system can be reformed rather than one sweeping programme for change. We see a set of moves in the right direction as more important than utopian blueprints and wishful thinking. We argue that these measures are not only realistic but also necessary if what we described as a problem is not to turn into a crisis that would see the further erosion and marginalization of social science in academia, the shrinking and closure of social science departments, and the continuing alienation of academics working in these fields. In this chapter, we address the identities of individual researchers and the research methodologies they use in their work, and encourage a different approach at the level of individual and group research practices and their outcomes. We argue for new scholarly identities and many different ways of fashioning them, in which research is one, but not the only, important practice. In Chapters 7 and 8 we will move on to address institutional and policy issues.

Our first priority must be a reorientation of social research away from the omnipresent requirement to continuously publish in 'high-quality' journals, to the overriding goal and ultimate purpose of creating original knowledge that matters to society. We seek, in other words, to shift the emphasis onto good and meaningful knowledge rather than the means of its dissemination. Journal publication is a *means* for facilitating the development, quality assurance, and communication of new knowledge, not an end in itself. It can be an effective means with certain advantages, but as we argued earlier, it is currently riven with problems. Therefore, the most important issue in getting social science back on track is to shift the emphasis away from massive paper production to the development of more innovative and resonant approaches and theories and—in particular—engaging texts that can make a significant difference to both theory and social practice. This would reduce mass publication to the benefit of more limited high-quality research publications.

An Emphasis on Meaningful Research

Key to addressing the problems is the cultivation of a very different orientation among individual academics from the one dominant today. Formal structures and arrangements here matter, but more important is cultural change. What individuals and groups of researchers choose to do matters. Compared to other professional groups, and even more so to employees outside the recognized professions, they enjoy considerable freedom in their work, both in how they organize their work and, more substantially, what their work is about. This includes the choice of frameworks, topics, methodologies, styles of writing, and publication outlets. Contrary to what we believe and sometimes feel, unlike many other occupational groups, as researchers we rarely experience brute power. What we do experience are institutional pressures and nudges, which we can choose to ignore or sidestep even if, in the short term at least, we may suffer some consequences.

To recover meaning in social research calls for reflection, dialogues with others, and self-criticism. It is, however, not particularly difficult for us as researchers to get some preliminary hints on whether we contribute meaningfully. We can start by persistently asking ourselves and each other five simple questions. These questions can feature regularly when we meet each other in seminars and conferences, when we review each other's submissions and books, and when we interview each other for appointments and promotions. All five questions are variations on the pressing and persistent overall question, *'So what?'*

- Have you got anything important to say to a qualified audience (outside your academic microtribe)?
- Would you say that this has not been said before or that you are not using new words to make an old point or that you are not just reproducing what we more or less already know or believe?

- Is this meaningful and socially relevant for others?
- Can you formulate a clear message with a novel idea or an insightful contribution summarizing your work within a minute or two?
- Is the value of what you have written and the time it took commensurate with your salary (compare for example with what nurses and primary school teachers earn)?

Those who can ask themselves these questions, and in particular the last one, and find meaningful answers without experiencing a sinking feeling or a strong urge to read aloud from their abstracts can feel some confidence that they have avoided manufacturing nonsense. But there is always a risk that one may deceive oneself. It is easy to exaggerate one's significance and relevance to others. Therefore, it is important to check if the answers to the questions above are confirmed by others. If these others do not turn their eyes away, or try to avoid the issues with various excuses, but say 'yes, definitively', then a researcher may feel a bit more confident about doing meaningful research.

Here, it is vital to consider who the 'others' are and their motives for a positive (or negative) response. One's friends and associates working within the same microtribe are unreliable. So too are all the 'yes-men' and 'yes-women' eager to be friendly and positive. Sometimes a group of practitioners or members of the public may find research good because it addresses broad and important questions and sets out to offer easy or, for the target group, politically convenient solutions. This may deceptively be perceived as meaningful.[1] However, the five questions about meaningful research should not be regarded as mere supplements to the usual line of critical questions posed during seminars and peer reviews. If a piece of research has no meaning, its rigour is of no value.

Cultivating a More Scholarly Identity: From Gap-Spotter to Path-(Up)Setter

Recovering meaning in social research calls for the development and nurturing of researcher identities, different from those constantly revolving around gap-spotting and journal hits. While changes in government, university, and journal policies—as we will discuss in Chapter 7—are all-important, they will not necessarily promote meaningful research unless academic identities and

---

[1] Of course, that an audience find a research project a good one is only one element in meaningful research. Precise research tasks, rigour, realism, and good empirical support are crucial. Weaknesses in these respects cannot be compensated for by the social relevance of research any more than rigour can make up for a socially meaningless research task.

norms of success and failure become redefined in fundamentally different ways. *The key here is to redefine ourselves and others as committed social scholars rather than as article-producing technicians.* This is one of the main themes of sociologist Gary T. Marx's (1990) essay 'Reflections on academic success and failure: Making it, forsaking it, reshaping it'. Marx describes the ephemerality and meaninglessness of academic success built on the back of journal hits and research grants. Committed social scholars see as their overall task having something meaningful—insightful, well grounded, and typically interesting—to say, and reaching a larger and broader audience than subspecialists. This commitment must be balanced with a strong sense of academic integrity: to refrain from following the party line, being politically correct, or simply reinforcing prefabricated interests. The agitator, like the technocrat, is alien to the ideal of a good scholar, even a socially committed one.

There are many different ways of being a scholar and, therefore, many different ways of earning the respect and admiration of one's peers, of which published outputs is but one. Being a scholar as an identity and a mode of working means *reading and thinking* more than managing data. It means arguing and engaging with the ideas of other scholars in written texts but also in conferences, seminars, and informal discussions. It means intervening in public debates and using scholarly arguments to dispel ideas bred from prejudice and ignorance. It means being a committed teacher, concerned about the education of future generations of citizens and also future scholars. It means being competent in certain techniques and methods of scientific inquiry, but also being wise in deploying them to meaningful ends and purposes. One can be a good scholar in different ways—by thinking alone or by collaborating with others, by doing qualitative or quantitative work, abstract or applied research, by concentrating on issues of teaching and pedagogy, or by reaching wider audiences through a variety of publications (including journalistic pieces, blogs, and so on) and fora. Being a scholar also means making a contribution to the different scientific communities and institutions as a socially involved citizen. Research is part of what it means to be a scholar, but the latter cannot be reduced to doing research, let alone to having journal hits.

To be a scholar one does not have to be a saint. Nor does one have to disown ambition, pride, and selfishness. But to be a scholar one has to shift from the mindset of research as a game to something more akin to Weberian vocation, where scholarship treats ideas and arguments as deadly serious rather than as a means of scoring in the publishing game and in career progression. Not all scholars can reach the highest ranks of the academy. But this is not a sign of failure. On the contrary. The vocation of being a scholar, like other vocations, calls for some sacrifices, and rapid career progression up the academic slippery pole may well be one of these sacrifices that true scholars are willing to make. Arguably, an emphasis on the meaningful rather than the profitable will often lead to a more satisfying working life, although not necessarily an easier and more comforting one.

Reading lies at the heart of being a scholar. Reading is time consuming and cannot be reduced to scanning the abstracts in a subfield and checking for keywords in Google Scholar. Scholarly reading means absorbing large parts of existing human knowledge seriously, interpreting them, and critiquing them. It is having a deep familiarity with thinkers and ideas not only within one's subfield but in social science at large. Reading over a long period of time is as important a part of a scholar's journey as his or her writing. Indeed, as Czarniawska (2004, p. 91) has argued, reading and writing are complementary ways of engaging with texts, complementing the question 'what does a text say?' with 'how does a text say it?' To develop his or her understanding, a scholar's reading needs to be diverse and progress over time. An academic who becomes an expert on a specific thinker and repeatedly reproduces and discusses what the hero(ine) has said and how it contributes to different fields of inquiry is not generally pursuing meaningful research. This is also the case irrespective of who the hero is—be it Milton Friedman, Max Weber, Michael Foucault, Karl Marx, or Judith Butler.

Both reading and writing engage a scholar's thinking capabilities and, if any development is to take place, this thinking must be *reflexive*. By this we mean that the thinking must also critically target itself, its own starting points, assumptions, lines of reasoning (initially or gradually) and indeed motives. Engagement and focus should be balanced with some degree of self-critique. The inclination to see things when you believe in them has to be tempered by a will to see also things that run counter to your beliefs and framework. The active cultivation and use of alternative points of departures, perspectives, and discourses can foster a degree of reflexivity where we are able to resist temptations to order reality in line with preconceptions and favoured ideas and concepts (Alvesson & Sköldberg, 2009). An important element in this reflexivity is to *acknowledge uncertainty and doubt* in the research process. This can also make papers and monographs more vivid and open for debate. Sadly, this is such a rare phenomenon among academics that one will look in vain for good examples. Yet, Locke et al. (2008) emphasize doubt as a key element in good research: cultivating doubt encourages you to think twice and be careful with the fatal tendency to always employ your favourite truth, your favourite guru, or your favourite formulaic jargon. Research should not just confirm and reproduce an established viewpoint, but aim for at least a degree of critiquing and challenging established knowledge. All this should be done with a consideration of the *social purpose* served by this thinking, reflection, and provocation.

In order to win back and cultivate a more scholarly, (self-)critical and innovative attitude among social researchers, cultural and identity issues must be directly addressed. Even if academic journals decide to emphasize meaningful research at the expense of technical excellence, the success of this will be dependent on a sufficient number of good researchers embracing this approach and learning to define themselves and their work in terms of a more socially committed scholarship. This is a task for all of us in academia. It is partly a matter of cultivating a specific self-understanding—through research choices, reflexive exercises, thoughtful (and not mainly gap-spotting instrumental) use of networks, collaborations, and so on, and partly in our capacity as PhD supervisors, colleagues, examiners, reviewers, and so on, to influence others. These institutional matters will be addressed in Chapter 7, but first we will take a closer look at some of the strategies the individual researcher can employ to return to meaning.

Polymorphic Research

As part of the identity recultivation, researchers could aim at what we call polymorphic research in contrast to the formulaic (Alvesson & Gabriel, 2013). Academic polymorphists are disinclined to stick to a specific locale. They are more like travellers seeking academic adventures than local specialists learning more and more about a specific habitat and its inhabitants. Polymorphic research involves:

A nomadic research trajectory, that is, moving between fields in order to attain cross-fertilization and the joys of serendipity. This can be found in practically all the canons of social science, notably in the works of Max Weber, Émile Durkheim, and Georg Simmel. Here, economics, religion, psychology, history, organization, and philosophy merge into theories that cannot be confined to any particular one of these disciplines. Similar research trajectories can be observed in eminent contemporary theorists such as Pierre Bourdieu, Axel Honneth, or David Graeber. It should be noticed that none of these scholars are in the 'application business'. A nomadic research trajectory cannot be reduced to 'applying Foucault' to family therapy or strategic management, or Deleuze to critical discourse analysis. This type of 'pairing together', which mostly amounts to writing footnotes to what others have already said, is rather a way of creating a niche for oneself in the gap-spotting business. Being nomadic is not to review one discipline from the perspective of another, but to take on the difficult task of having something to say which is relevant to each of them.

Nomads are not in all places at the same time. They move from place to place, sometimes rapidly, at other times deliberately. Such journeys are not without risks and disappointments but after a few years, nomads find themselves in new locations quite different from earlier ones. At that point, they can move back to an earlier location—with the capacity to say something new. Researchers who remain in the same arena for ten years or more, rather than taking pride in their 'dedication', should feel some embarrassment about their lack of adventure and their preference for the comforts of habits or doing 'roisearch'. It is time to break out of the knowledge box—the longer one stays, the more difficult it becomes to avoid a 'boxed-in' knowledge position, where networks, capacity, working style, mindset, habits, and identity all become frozen and expert-like rather than scholarly (Alvesson & Sandberg, 2014).

Scholarly movements are not restricted to moves across research terrains (theories, phenomena, methods), but also include what type of text you produce and which group you interact with. *Aiming for nonstandardized text production* both within the confinements of scientific journals and in other genres, is therefore essential to being a polymorphic researcher. At the moment, three genres dominate social science: the formulaic journal article, the formulaic monograph, and the formulaic textbook. Needless to say, these genres do exhibit examples of 'real' texts illustrating both what it means to have an original message and a clear voice. But this is rare. By sticking to the dominant formats social scientists are letting themselves appear squarer than they actually are—or at least could be. As one of our colleagues, a very charming person, was told by a student. 'You, and many other professors, are such a humoristic, engaged and charming person in real life, but none of that comes through in your publications. These are rather boring and lifeless.' So true and so unnecessary, we think.

Other genres, such as essays, pamphlets, stories, blogs, and chronicles are, depending on the material, often more efficient and aesthetically pleasing to read. Within the academic book genre, one might refer to Sennett (1998) or Kunda (1992) which both read as novels without losing in descriptive quality or analytic precision. But also the 1000-word chronicle can, with some humour and a punchline, often be exemplary. The apprehension that these formats restrain researchers from the 'academically sound' in terms of rigour and reflexive balance is a bad excuse for not developing the versatility of one's writing skills. Scholars have different obligations than the average pundit. Their opinions cannot simply be 'opinions' without foundation in research that they and others have pursued. The only reason why this should prevent them from taking part in the general debate is because they have not done their homework.

Even if it means popularizing and simplifying what one has to say, *interaction with the nonspecialized public* both helps individual researchers to develop a polymorphic research trajectory, and to make their research socially meaningful. Here, natural science might serve as an inspiration. The extent to which scientists such as Brian Cox, Richard Dawkins, Stephen Hawking, and Steven Rose have managed to engage in public debate has very few counterparts in the whole of social science. Although they do exist, they are remarkably few given that society, after all, is subject to considerably more debate than physics and biology. The ones we have left, such as Noam Chomsky, Jürgen Habermas, Zygmunt Bauman, and Amartya Sen, belong to a generation for whom the pressure on—and availability of templates for—formulaic publishing and an inclination to be an academic subspecialist was very different from today. A few somewhat younger economists like Paul Krugman and Joseph Stieglitz are, although more specialist and narrow, also exceptions. Finding a form for 'reaching out' is in itself an art—simply stating that we will start making social science 'public', as in the case of Burawoy, is clearly not enough. The idea is not for all academics to try to be world celebrities, we are only mentioning big names because they may be familiar to the reader. Yet it is fully possible to reach a national or local audience or a part of the public that has a clear interest in certain issues.

Writing is key for a recovery of meaning in research. In Chapter 5 we pointed at the massive problems of academic writings discouraging non-specialists from reading the text. A writer interested in reaching a broader audience shows a lot of care not only for those who decide over publication—editors and reviewers—but also the decision makers, professional practitioners, or members of the educated public that may have limited tolerance for jargon, abstract texts, the bad habit of inserting references as often as possible, and producing formulaic texts which are more or less standardized, impersonal, and cautious. Writing needs to try to attract and to keep attention, to have something important to say, and to make the reader feel that this is the mission of the author. Texts that are well written, possibly with some humour, perhaps including some personal elements, that use unexpected and provocative language and appeal to the reader's curiosity, are important. This is difficult to accomplish. One must allow oneself a freer tone, but even more—one must read and be inspired by good examples and then work intensively with the crafting and recrafting of the text. One needs to let go the ideal of an academic text as an 'impenetrable fortress', written in such an uninviting and apparently foolproof way so that no one feels inclined to see any shortcomings or targets for attack. Occasionally, authors manage to write as if the research publication has some of the qualities of good fiction or an ambitious journalistic article. This does not have to be at the expense of empirical precision or well-grounded interpretations and insights. On the contrary, social phenomena need good textual support to highlight points and here a variety of writing styles need to be considered and developed (van Maanen 1988, 1995).

The polymorphic ideal may seem distant to PhD students or junior lecturers struggling to launch their careers. Younger researchers normally have to work a couple of years within a subfield and master it before moving along to other fields. They need to learn to write one type of text before developing a variety of styles and formats. They also need to test their ideas before seeking to reach a broader audience. But these dangers that the polymorphic idea poses to young scholars should not prevent others from venturing beyond their narrow habitats, specializing in one type of writing and only addressing academics within their microtribe. It is both possible and fundamental to have research interests outside one's major project, to spend some time and energy writing for other outlets than the (formulaic) dissertation or journal paper and to talk about your research to different audiences and make an effort to demonstrate that it is interesting and meaningful. Some scholars may do these things spontaneously, but they can also be cultivated. They can be viewed as part of an identity project: we are—or become—our intellectual trajectories (or standstills), our writings and our key relations and interactions. For these reasons, we believe that the polymorphic ideal should become part of a researcher's identity project at an early career stage.

These themes (movements across fields, diversity of writing genres, diversity of audiences, constant monitoring of the meaning of one's efforts) can become embedded in the reflexive practices of individual researchers but also central to the collective practices of research groups, conferences, and departments as part of (a) self-scrutiny, (b) seminar and review culture, (c) institutional support through workshops and advice-giving and (d) employment and promotion discussions.

Two Methodologies for Doing Interesting Research

If social research is to rediscover its social meaning and purpose, one of the first things it must do is to move swiftly away from the arid, unimaginative, and formulaic patterns of vacuum-cleaning the literature in a particular field, identifying a gap, and then setting off to fill it with the aid of a formulaic methodology, either qualitative or quantitative (and very rarely a combination of these two). Earlier, we criticized such methodologies for producing incremental, formulaic, and usually meaningless results. Instead of viewing 'methodology' as a set of techniques that mechanically and reliably deliver supposedly rigorous knowledge, we view methodology as a set of ideas and practices on how to carry out research including theoretical and empirical work. Methodology, by itself, cannot deliver meaningful knowledge in social science, but imaginative methodologies are more likely to generate interesting and potentially useful results. We therefore present two methodologies to this end: using problematization as a means of challenging assumptions; and using empirical material to generate new ideas and theories departing from and challenging existing literature (for other examples, see Abbott, 2004; Becker, 1998). Both emphasize theoretical novelty. Novel and interesting research may not necessarily be of social value, but only by being interesting to a wider public can it reach beyond the narrow confines of academic micro-tribes and rapid oblivion. Interestingness is not everything, but it is a key element in getting attention and making an impact. This is crucial for social science, as it needs to be read and listened to. Of course, there is the risk that interesting research will not be entirely meaningful and not all meaningful research needs to be interesting, but avoidance of repetition and marginal adding to what many have said already is crucial. And interestingness is often a key element in meaningful research, so considering this will be a big step in the right direction. The two methodologies presented here are only intended as illustrations, since this book does not aim to provide a full methodological overview. The two examples take specific issue with the fundamental problems of mainstreaming, incrementalism, and shortage of novelty in contemporary social science.

Using problematization as a methodology for assumption-challenging studies. An alternative to fine-tuning knowledge by filling tiny gaps is to formulate research questions by questioning and undermining, in short 'problematizing', some dominant assumptions in existing research. As Davis (1971) has argued in his famous paper 'That's interesting', this is what opens up rich opportunities to generate interesting ideas, concepts, and theories. Problematization of existing assumptions is a fruitful way of formulating novel research questions and is not just the same as criticizing the assumptions of others from one's preferred meta-theoretical standpoint, something that is normal in cross-paradigm debates and disputes and in various applications of critical perspectives (Alvesson & Sandberg, 2013). Such ready-made or 'pseudo-problematization' only reproduces the researcher's own assumptions and is unlikely to lead to particularly novel and interesting ideas. Real problematization involves identifying one's own assumptions, including those underlying one's meta-theoretical position, and submitting them to critical scrutiny by persistently asking the question, 'What if?' The ambition is not to totally undermine one's position, but only to destabilize it sufficiently to enable the asking of novel and probing research questions.

The aim of placing problematization at the heart of methodology is, as Abbott puts it, 'to come up with novel research questions through a *dialectical interrogation* of one's own familiar position, other stances, and the domain of literature targeted for assumption challenging'. This approach supports a more reflective-scholarly attitude in the sense that it encourages the researcher to start 'using different standard stances to question one another...[and combining them] into far more complex forms of questioning than any one of them can produce alone' (Abbott, 2004, p. 87).

To be able to problematize assumptions through such a dialectical interrogation, the following methodological principles are useful: (1) identify a domain of literature; (2) identify and articulate assumptions underlying this domain; (3) evaluate them; (4) develop an alternative assumption ground; (5) consider it in relation to its audience; and (6) evaluate the alternative assumption ground. Beyond such general principles, however, successful problematization is very much a matter of creativity, intuition, reading inspiring texts that offer critical insights, and as noted above asking the question 'What if' where connections and arguments seem self-evident. Problematization cannot be reduced to a sequence of rational, logical, or mechanistic procedures, but rather can be developed as the systematic quality of a restless and inquiring mind which is neither kowtowed by academic convention nor deterred by the prospect of many fruitless attempts and mental experiments. Such a quality has the advantage of becoming embedded in a research identity that reaches beyond a mere gap-spotter without lapsing in to the adolescent delight of constantly playing devil's advocate. (This methodology is extensively developed and exemplified in Alvesson & Sandberg, 2013.)

Identifying and solving mysteries in empirical research. A second methodology for generating novel and interesting theories is by challenging the links between empirical material and theoretical conclusions. Many researchers approach what is assumed to be robust quantitative or qualitative data (generated through grounded theory, experiments, ethnographies, observations, and so forth) as both the basis for delivering theoretical insights through proper analysis and as the final arbiter of their theories' truthfulness. We, by contrast, do not regard empirical material as the royal road to theory or interesting insights, no matter how diligently and rigorously it has been collected and how technically well it has been analysed. Inductive approaches like grounded theory suffer from a codification obsession, and seldom take off boldly and imaginatively from reformulations of pattern findings (Alvesson and Sköldberg 2009). Instead, we see theory and empirical material in a constant interplay with the latter as a source of inspiration rather than as the ultimate arbiter for the latter. Theory and empirical material must be in constant dialogue, interrogating and refining each other, with special attention being paid to discontinuities, paradoxes, and mysteries. We consequently suggest a methodology for theory development through encounters between theoretical assumptions and empirical impressions that highlight breakdowns. It is the unanticipated and the unexpected—the anomalies that puzzle the researcher—that are of particular interest in the encounter. Accordingly, theory development is stimulated and facilitated through a special interest in what does *not* work in an existing theory or in received wisdom. The ideal of this research methodology can be summed up as including two elements: the identification of a mystery, and its solution (Alvesson and Kärreman, 2011; Asplund, 1970).

This ideal is *not*, as in neo-positivist work, to aim for an 'intimate interaction with actual evidence' that 'produces theory which closely mirrors reality' (Eisenhardt, 1989, p. 547). Aiming to mirror reality, we believe, hampers the imagination and usually produces low-abstraction, context-specific, and trivial results. Of course, theories need to be empirically tested and supported in order to be seen as trustworthy and valuable. As many empiricists, not least Milgram and Asch in psychology, and Durkheim in sociology, would acknowledge, reality-mirroring needs be balanced by other criteria, such as the ability to point at deep structures or hidden meanings (not so easy to capture in a mirror), and to offer novel interpretations and develop ideas, concepts, and lines of reasoning that enhance our ability to think in different ways about social reality and open up new possibilities of understanding. As with problematization, the aim of creating and solving mysteries is to generate more imaginative, interesting, and socially relevant knowledge. This often means not discovering new things about the world, but seeing old things with fresh eyes and fresh mindsets. (For an extensive description and exemplification of this methodology, see Alvesson & Kärreman, 2011.)

The two methodologies proposed here are not just different techniques for doing social science research—they represent different intellectual orientations towards the research effort and different approaches to knowledge and understanding. They call for scholarship that draws on a broader set of theories and vocabularies as resources to challenge dominant theoretical assumptions and constructions of empirical material, more emphasis on critical and hermeneutic interpretations, and some boldness in questioning consensus. This means a less obsessive emphasis on all detailed 'findings' and knowledge within narrowly defined fields, a reluctance to divide up theory and data as separate categories, and a willingness to deal with some antagonism from defenders of established positions, even at some cost to one's career. Given the fundamental problem of replicating even experimental studies, some reduction of the faith in empiricism and some upgrading of empirical work as a means for generating and revising ideas, insights, and theories and to think further seems motivated. An alternative to the offering of final truths, that is, carefully verified hypotheses, is to see social science as offering empirically supported frameworks, concepts, ideas, and so forth, that aid our thinking and reflections as scholars, professionals, and intellectually interested citizens.

To repeat, there is nothing essential in these methodological ideas that guarantees meaningful social research. But the emphasis on avoiding the reproduction of established frameworks and findings and attempts to give priority to new, unexpected ideas and insights go some way in the direction of having something to say, potentially also to an audience outside the researcher's microtribe. Such an audience often asks for some intellectual excitement. Hence, the methodologies need to be supplemented with the selection of socially relevant research tasks, and should work with the development and communication of ideas and findings that can appeal to a broader audience.

Recovering Meaning in Teaching

Recovering meaning in social research—doing interesting, socially relevant, and accessible research—as advocated above, is part of the ideal of a socially committed scholar. This scholar is eager to have something meaningful to say not only to academic peers but also to his/her wider audience. This audience includes students, perhaps the most significant target group of research. Socially committed scholars neither construct their identities nor assess their self-worth solely on the back of the numbers of publications they can boast or the citations that these attract. As we mentioned earlier, there are many ways of being a good scholar. Passing on knowledge, and the skills of learning and researching to the younger generations has always been a part of the vocation of the scholar, and is one that we believe must be revalorized.

One of the direst consequences of the overproduction of research publications has been the gradual debasement and degradation of teaching as part of the life world of academics. In virtually every academic institution where research takes place, teaching is viewed as an inferior activity to that of writing and publishing. Academics whose work is defined principally by teaching see their careers suffer, their time cluttered with administrative responsibilities, and their own sense of self-esteem and identity undermined. Teaching is now sometimes seen as a *punishment* for being unsuccessful in research. Many successful researchers end up viewing teaching time as time stolen from research. And yet, compared to the contribution to society made by teaching, the contribution made by volumes of unread article journals is minimal. The academic time spent in producing these articles, reviewing them, editing them, revising them, and publishing them seems to produce less value than time spent in preparing lectures and seminars, keeping up to date with pedagogical practices, developing teaching materials, including case studies, tests, videos, online materials and so forth, marking students' work diligently, and offering pastoral care and counselling to students. It is our belief, therefore, that unless and until teaching resumes its critical place (along with research) in the self-identities of scholars, many of the problems identified in this book will escalate. The rift that is currently emerging between students, becoming ever more needy, demanding, and dissatisfied, and academics who see themselves as constantly pestered by students, bombarded with unwelcome emails and deflected from their valuable writing time, will widen.

There are many factors that contribute to the current overvaluation of research and under-valuation of teaching. Institutional prestige is rarely won on the back of outstanding teaching, pedagogy, or caring for students. By contrast, research performance (including citation scores) and other metrics, including the employability of graduates, dominate the reputational standings of different universities. Furthermore, most universities have long turned a blind eye to ineffective teachers, as long as they were able to earn sizeable research grants or to deliver prestigious research outputs. Individual researchers who spend inordinate amounts of time revising and resubmitting papers in pursuit of the Holy Grail of seeing their name in a starred journal are seldom going to be criticized for wasting their time (and arguably taxpayers' or students' money). Nor are reviewers pouring over manuscripts for the nth time and requesting the (n+1)th revision of authors, splitting hairs and micro-managing the text, likely to be chastised for taking time away from the pastoral care of students or citizenship duties—indeed, they may maintain that requesting yet another revision is precisely what their citizenship duties demand.

Currently, there is some indication that teaching, the Cinderella of work in research-led institutions, is experiencing some renaissance, at least in some countries, where student evaluations of teaching in institutional and national surveys is assuming a higher profile. In the UK, the National Student Survey is open to all final-year undergraduate students who are invited to comment on the quality of their courses, including the quality of teaching, of organization and management, of assessment and feedback, of career advice and pastoral care, and so forth. It started in 2005 and has quickly become a powerful institution which universities as well as prospective students take very seriously. Response rates have increased over the years and currently stand at over 80 per cent of all those eligible. One of this book's authors has had ample opportunities to observe how even minor declines in a department's standing in this survey can prompt widespread alarm and prompt corrective measures. Individual departments in virtually every UK university are now following the example of US universities in inviting their students to rate their professors on a number of different metrics. Dropping below a particular standard in these measures precipitates some corrective action (usually a 'talk' with the associate dean responsible for teaching, followed by an offer of training courses and peer support and counselling). There is some evidence that falling below particular standards may jeopardize a young academic's chances of a permanent job in a research-active institution.

Failures in teaching rarely have the damaging effect on the careers of young academics that failure to publish can have. Yet, there is evidence that teaching will continue to rise on the agenda. Many academics will experience this renewed emphasis on teaching as unwelcome—yet more pressure to perform, yet more distraction from their valuable writing time. We, however, welcome this. We believe that recovering the meaning of teaching will support the recovery of meaning in social research. The cross-fertilization of teaching and research at the heart of academic identities will help restore an ideal of scholarship that prevailed over many centuries before it was eroded by the forces we analysed in Part I of this book, and the rise of the publishing game as the major institution governing academic careers and selfhood.

In Conclusion

At a recent conference in which many critical views on the current meaning of scholarship were aired, a senior academic came up with a striking analogy. To be a scholar, he argued, is like being a decathlete, an individual with a fundamental athleticism but capable of channelling it in a variety of events and disciplines. Reducing scholarship to journal publications is like turning a decathlon competition into a pole vaulting event, a highly skilled event but not one in which every decathlete can excel. The analogy was greeted with much approval by the conference audience. In this chapter we have advocated a recovery of meaning in social research by restoring the ideal of a scholar at the heart of academic practices and identities, and by seeking to supplant the dominance of the publishing game as the main arbiter of academic worth. We argued that there are many different ways of being a scholar and these should be valued and acknowledged. All of these ways involve both research and teaching. With regard to research, we proposed a number of practices and methodologies that we believe will enhance the value of social science knowledge for the rest of society, make it more interesting to non-specialists and enhance its relevance and impact on wider society. With regard to teaching, we advocated its revalorization and re-incorporation into the ideal of scholarship, its higher profile in hiring and promotion decisions, and an absolute end to the mentality that casts it as a penalty for failure in research. Above all, we sought to emphasize that academics have many more choices in how they conduct their work as professionals and how they construct their own identities through their work.

Unlike most jobs, social science researchers are privileged with having many choices: what to study, what methodologies to use, who to choose as their allies and their opponents, where to try and publish their work, what journals and books to read and what to ignore, who to collaborate with, what funding to seek, and what meetings to attend. They can also choose how much of their personal life and time to dedicate to their research, how to handle boundaries between work and leisure, scholarship and family life. They can also often decide if they want to be very research active—although this may call for hard work in getting grants or being flexible in joining research teams—or want to focus on teaching and administration, and perhaps voluntarily reduce research time for other tasks. In making such choices, the work of social science researchers can end up defining them and anchoring their identities. But many academics downplay the freedom they have in constructing their identity and emphasize the imperatives and pressures, something that is exacerbated when they find themselves immersed in publishing games whose outcomes they cannot control. Recovering meaning in social research in the ways we have indicated in this chapter seeks to reinstate identity as a crucial part of the research, not as the product of external pressures but as the result of the researchers' own conscious (and sometimes unconscious) choices and the ways they exercise their freedoms. Here the option of an academic teacher may be optimal for many people finding research and publishing difficult, or less rewarding.

The chapters that follow offer some suggestions on how institutional and policy levels can support the proposals made in this chapter.

7

Recovering Meaning by Reforming Organizations and Institutions

In this chapter we address what universities, university departments, and professional institutions can do to support the recovery of meaning in social research. We examine how the practices of journals, publishers, conference organizers, workshops, and other research-related institutions can be reformed to this end. We also look at how departmental and school practices can be reformed. These include PhD training, other research-relevant educational matters, seminars, workshops, and promotion. Of course, universities as well as publishers, conference organizers, and other research institutions also involve administrative hierarchies and staff, policies, rules, and regulations. Although there is evidence that the influence of administrative and support staff has been increasing in many universities, they are not the principal determinants of how communities of academics behave. It is academics themselves, and in particular senior academics, who are generally in control as deans, departmental heads, editors, conference organizers, and policy makers.

Professional Communities Reclaiming Meaning

Professional communities are the dominant norm-setters for researchers. Research is generally conducted by 'cosmopolitans', that is, individuals whose main audiences are made up of an international community of peers (Gouldner, 1957). Some researchers may also focus on local, regional, and national matters, addressing their specific issues and problems. Most of them, however, would seek to support their arguments and their findings with evidence and theories obtained across countries, and will also see themselves as members of microtribes that cross organizational and national frontiers.

Professional associations and more loosely structured communities often organize conferences, workshops, and other gatherings as well as courses. They also run journals, have newsletters and, sometimes, book series. That publishers own and manage the operational side of journals does not alter the fact that their content and practices are in the hands of academics. Publishers have little say on what is published and what type of research is privileged in a specific journal. Hence, we will address journals as run and governed by academics, including editors, authors, associate editors, and reviewers. We believe that there is a great deal that these academics can do at the organizational and institutional levels to promote meaningful social science research.

Rethinking Professional Norms: Journals and Other Publication Forms

Rethinking professional norms in relation to journal publications should be one of the primary concerns in recovering meaning for social research. We recognize that there is a great variety of journals in social science, each adopting slightly different practices from the others in its field. Some disciplines are in many countries pluralistic (for example, management, sociology, education), while others tend to be more homogenous (for example, economics, psychology). However, we feel that in the same way that formulaic publications have come to dominate academic publishing, many journals seem to aspire to the same formula of what constitutes a successful, prestigious journal. These stress rigorous blind review procedures, highly specialized articles addressed to microtribes, uniform conventions on methodologies and literature reviews, an increasing tendency to disperse editorial responsibility to numerous joint editors and associate editors, a tendency to promote special issue pampering to the needs of microtribes, and a fetishization of impact factors as a measure of a journal's value and worth. The suggestions that follow are not meant to further reduce the diversity of journals available in social science. On the contrary, we would advocate a greater diversity of journals, appealing to a diversity of audiences, using different types of articles and approaches, different presentations, and different ways of enhancing their quality. What we believe, however, is that a much higher emphasis should be accorded to publishing texts that have something meaningful and valuable to say to a wider audience than most journals are currently doing.

As noted earlier, over a couple of decades, publishing academic papers, especially in high-impact or high-prestige journals, has come to dominate every other aspect of research, something reflected in how academics present themselves on university web pages and author biographies. Journals have a vital role to play in social research and in academic life in general, and in certain ways international publications based on peer reviews can increase meaningfulness through countering bad quality research written for a local or national audience. Nevertheless, journal publication has become far too dominant. This is widely recognized and, as we noted earlier, it tends to create conservative, incremental, highly technical, and generally 'low-meaning' publications. Many researchers seem concerned only to get their paper accepted by satisfying reviewers, even at what cost. They follow slavishly reviewers' and editors' instructions, even if this dilutes their argument, takes them off on irrelevant detours, or inflates their articles to often ridiculous lengths. Of course, following reviewers' requests can lead to significant improvements, but often reviewers have criteria other than those of meaningfulness and relevance for a potentially broader audience. A meaningful social science is undermined by the over-emphasis on journal publication, of the adaptation to specialized reviewers, and of the strong trend to homogenous and formulaic styles of reviewing and publishing.

One can imagine radically revised types of *texts and contributions* than the ones that now dominate most academic fields. Among editors, non-formulaic qualities could be stimulated rather than eliminated. The 'so what' question, which is seldom asked today, should be among the first editors start with. One could even say that this is the key question. A clear answer should be expected—and a more satisfying answer than one of filling the gap in the literature or adding (marginally) to (existing) theory should be asked for. Originality in style and structure, the paper's broader appeal, and practical and policy ramifications should balance the concern about 'rigour'. Polymorphic formats, like essays, reflections on practice, and dialogues across disciplinary frontiers, that are now little more than appendices to the 'real' articles, can be elevated to 'normal business' leaving the special sections for formulaic research. Accessible, lean texts, stripped of excessive jargon, unnecessary references, lengthy method sections, and vacuum-cleaning literature reviews, could be encouraged and rewarded. A realistic ambition for most scholarly journals in social science would be that at least half the papers should be relevant and comprehensible outside specific academic microtribes.

The *review process* can also be changed to the same end. A major step forward would be to limit the number of revisions to two before a firm editorial decision on whether to publish or not is made. This would forestall the 'escalation of commitment' dynamic which locks reviewers and authors into a process usually ending up in tepid and overlong articles or bitter and costly rejections. A limited number of revisions would also encourage authors and reviewers to be firmer in holding their ground and editors to use their editorial judgement rather than in deferring to yet another round of reviews. An adherence to word limits would have the same effect—restricting unrealistic reviewers' expectations driven by the 'Would it not be interesting if...?' mentality which usually leads to unnecessary excursions into areas that authors have no interest whatsoever in pursuing. A related measure would be limiting the number of references and citations, only permitting references to sources with whose work an author actively engages rather than a litany of names ostensibly strengthening an argument, in reality placating or anticipating the objections of reviewers or signalling an authors' likes and dislikes. The reduction in the size of references and citations would put an end to the current practice of completing virtually every second sentence of academic articles with a string of names and dates, and would greatly enhance the readability of articles. One possibility that many journals may consider, is to include non-expert reviewers and invite them to judge how relevant or interesting a paper is from their non-specialist perspective. These could be high-quality journalists, or professional practitioners in areas including policy-making, politics, social reform, politicians, and managers known for thoughtfulness and intellectual interests.

Certainly, the majority of all submissions will need to be rejected and others will need to be substantially revised. Indeed, we have read many articles of doubtful value that have been published even in so-called A-listed journals. We are not advocating more generousity in journal publishing, but the opposite. It is of course impossible to find a formula for the optimal review and acceptance criteria for journal publication. But one can envisage journals upgrading innovative and original ideas (a consequence would be rejecting many more papers than currently, on that criterion) and/or a strong empirical contribution, and to be more relaxed about papers following a formula for a good paper. Upon receiving the first draft, it is often easy to tell whether or not the contribution is strong. If the contribution is strong, then let authors treat reviewers' comments as collegial advice for how to develop their work, rather than as strict instructions on what to do. Reviewers should then be less concerned with details and improvements and instead mainly focus on if the paper has a clear contribution to socially relevant and meaningful knowledge. This procedure could also be more open and transparent as we suggest below. This does not mean low standards. On the contrary, a good idea is demanding, and a convincing answer to the 'so what' question would imply an upgrading of some criteria. In other words, we are proposing a strengthening of some criteria and a relaxation of others.

Another criterion for evaluating submitted papers that needs to be reconsidered is the conventional notion of *rigour*, requesting researchers to systematically micro-distil existing literature in order to demonstrate how their own study makes a contribution to that literature and to devote much energy to coding and other modes of data management. This kind of 'mechanical' rigour is often used as the prime guillotine for rejecting a paper in the review process. This may be justifiable but it can also work against innovative and interesting approaches. Rigour and imagination do not have to be rivals (for example, Cornelissen and Floyd, 2009; Weick, 1989). However, conventional rigour in the sense of logical consistency and thoroughness generally encourages a refinement of existing theories and a normalization of quantification as the ideal, rather than the development of more frame-breaking and socially meaningful theories. This works against the study of rich but ad hoc cases like those favoured by journalists and thinkers such as Barbara Ehrenreich, Naomi Klein, Gary Greenberg, or George Monbiot whose work offers generous insights without having to fit the straightjacket of methodological rigour. Some social science academics, like Burawoy, Sennett, and Bauman can follow the same path, especially if they are already established and do not seek to be published in 'top journals'. But the vast majority of academics would not even consider this type of inquiry into a complex and ambiguous reality, as it is difficult to discipline through conventional methodologies and ideas of 'rigour'.

Another way of escaping from the methodological straightjacket without abandoning rigorous thinking would be to request authors to *identify their assumptions and specify those that they seek to question or challenge*, as suggested in Chapter 6. In other words, journals could request authors to carefully consider the assumptions underlying existing literature, and how those assumptions shape the understanding and conceptualization of the subject in question, thus making reflexivity a quality of rigorous thinking (Alvesson et al., 2008). There are many different ways of creating meaningful and valuable texts in social science once the straightjacket of methodological rigour has been loosened, including well-crafted empirical texts based on 'thick description' (Geertz, 1973) conveying insightful experiences that share many qualities with good fiction. Such texts evoke understanding that represents virtues other than good data management and sound number crunching. Again, we are not against the latter. Quantification is necessary and valuable for many research purposes, but neither she nor her less developed qualitative sister, coding, represent the only ways of doing meaningful social science research.

Before leaving the topic of journal publishing, we should draw attention to special issues, a common phenomenon capable of generating considerable insights and offering much value both to particular research communities and to wider society. A special issue, when properly conceived and executed, can radically shift the research agenda, place important and under-represented issues on the map, carve up new territories for exploration, and permit marginalized and silenced areas an opportunity to be heard. For all these reasons, we favour special issues when they are in character with a journal's mission and philosophy. All the same, we must caution against the use of special issues as devices for ever more esoteric and meaningless publishing, for academic micro-favours and for turning microtribes into academic communities. There is also the matter of opportunism—many academics relabel what they do in order to be able to submit to an SI (often viewed as easier to get accepted by).

The choice of subjects for special issues must be made with great care—obviously such subjects must have a strong and persuasive group of advocates or champions. Before accepting an SI, such champions may be invited to demonstrate the social value of their topic, its significance beyond their narrow specialization, and the potential for cross-fertilization with other traditions. The reviewers of articles submitted to special issues should not be drawn narrowly from specialists and enthusiasts; the articles selected for publication should demonstrate their value to a wider range of scholars. Editors of an SI should make an extra effort to locate the contributions they select within a wider social agenda, and present the articles they publish as parts of an evolving conversation which seeks to include, rather than to exclude, non-specialists. In all these ways, we believe that special issues, when handled with care, offer a sound opportunity for the kind of scholarship advocated in this book.

Rethinking Professional Norms: Conferences, Seminars, and Workshops

Academic conferences, seminars, and workshops have long been important features of academic life. Opportunities for scholars to meet formally and informally, to present their arguments and have them scrutinized and debated, to familiarize themselves with current trends and debates in their discipline, are all tried and tested means of promoting research and so it should be. The unofficial business of such meeting places is also important, not least as means of enhancing occupational norms and practices. In recent decades, however, there has been a tendency for conferences and workshops to turn into rehearsal grounds for the launch and testing of formulaic papers and for avid behind-the-scenes canvassing to obtain favourable conditions for submitted papers. In addition, 'Meet the editors' sessions have turned into highlights of such conferences—at a recent management conference in Paris more people turned out for these sessions than for the formal plenaries, the reason being obvious. Attending plenaries may expose one to some of the brightest minds in one's field but does not make the publication of papers any easier. By contrast, 'Meet the editors' sessions are currently treated by many scholars, especially young ones, as sacred occasions for receiving the word from the mouth of the oracle. Editors for their part, especially those of more prestigious journals, use these sessions as opportunities to promote themselves, but also to enhance a highly formulaic approach to research. 'If you wish to be published in my journal', they proclaim, 'you need to tick Boxes A, B, C and D.' Rarely is there a box ticked for promoting meaningful and socially valuable knowledge. One question for assessment could be: is this a paper you'd like your intelligent neighbour interested in the subject matter (municipality politics, whistleblowing, health care work) to read?

It would be unrealistic to expect that many of the less reputable practices encountered in academic conferences (instrumental networking, dubious deals, endemic flattery, and backscratching) will vanish overnight. There is, however, evidence that conference organizers themselves are becoming concerned by the limited social relevance of their activities and are considering ways of reforming their meetings and the publications under their supervision. In this way, for example, the European Academy of Management has initiated a series of debates on reforming its own publications and conferences. It is also seeking to use its influence on accrediting bodies to encourage scholarship on the burning social issues of our times, such as poverty, inequality, sustainability, and the mass movement of populations. A great many voices are currently being heard censuring the absurdities resulting from the fetishization of rankings and lists, and looking for ways to encourage research that will reconnect scholars and practitioners in mutually beneficial dialogue.

Opening Science to Public Scrutiny

As was brutally revealed by the Open Science Collaboration in 2015, experimental psychologists who are particularly close to natural science with their focus on statistical 'evidence', do not live up to their own standards of reproducibility. Now that two studies have demonstrated that experimental economics also fail in this respect (see Chapter 5), the endeavour to open up science to other researchers, and—we would add—to public scrutiny, appears more relevant than ever. The open science movement, most associated with psychologist Brian Nosek (see OSC, 2012, 2015), does not only offer new ways of making social science more reliable and accountable for its results. It can also push it in a more collaborative and meaningful direction.

There are primarily three institutional changes that recur in the debates on open science. The first, and most fundamental, concerns the *empirical work* and the openness of data collection. The whole process from gathering experiment data, survey data, interview material, or ethnographic material, to the writing of a journal article or monograph is normally closed to everyone outside the research team. Only rarely are others invited to look at raw data or at interview transcriptions for instance. This means that a lot can happen during the 'data management' that might reflect badly on the published results, or even contradict them. As a supplement to reproducing studies that others have already conducted, opening up the empirical work would mean a radical amount of transparency, but also a possibility for closer peer review. Whenever a new experimental project is embarked upon, the results could easily be made public in the same moment they are registered by connecting them to open data journals that are accessible to everyone. This would mean no delay and minimal risk of file drawer effects and manipulation of data. Naturally, due to ethical concerns about confidentiality, such openness is more difficult to attain in qualitative research, but there is no reason why all qualitative material should remain as closed as today once transcriptions and field notes have been taken and names made anonymous. A good example of how qualitative material could be made accessible is the ESDS Qualidata archive that provides access to a wide range of qualitative material in the UK. Sharing one's qualitative material would invite others to study whether quotations and accounts are taken from their proper context, and whether interpretations and conclusions that have been drawn are fair and well anchored. It would also allow radical coding triangulation, elaboration on the material, and increased opportunity to discover new patterns and meanings in it. Considering how little that normally comes out after years of empirical work, and the widely shared sense that one could have used the material to address other issues than the ones one finally settled on, this could give way to a more lively research process and meaningful utilization of empirical material.

There are, however, some problems with this, in particular in qualitative research. It emphasizes strongly the formal procedure and the need to carefully transcribe interviews and to store it in systematic ways. All this is time consuming and expensive. Often it may be wiser for a researcher to spend less time on extensive data management than doing more interviews, perhaps interviewing the same subjects several times and getting deeper or richer accounts. Sometimes it may be wise to be selective in terms of their use—often interviews are of low quality as interviewees lack verbal skills and/or motivation to provide rich and reliable accounts (Alvesson, 2011). In many cases qualitative studies need to rely more on the researcher's judgement, than on the ability to sort data. Often qualitative research depends on the researcher having 'been there' and having a strong feeling for the local context—abstract interview quotes may be difficult to grasp and if they are taken at face value they may be misleading. The qualitative interview is typically an interactional accomplishment and difficult to access without a strong sense of the context. In addition, qualitative material is often used to get insights, not just mirror or summarize the statements of interviewees, and if all material is accessible for scrutiny by others, it may make researchers cautious and inclined to focus only on staying close to data and then not saying much as this may lead to risks for misrepresenting data. A final reservation concerns the low likelihood of other researchers going through extensive, carefully transcribed interview material. In the worst case, much effort is spent in developing extensive databases, which are afterwards hardly used. Regardless of these difficulties, it is rather crucial that qualitative material becomes more attainable to reviewers and the public. Unless qualitative researchers develop a more transparent way of analysing their data, 'rigour' will have to remain a concept merely describing how good the black box looks on the outside. Analyses based on intuitions, feelings, and interviews that no one except the author has access to, might with some willpower be considered 'research'—but not 'science'.

While opening up the empirical work may require large institutional change and extra resources, there are less demanding changes that could be implemented tomorrow. One such change is to open up *the peer-review process*. Today, once an article or monograph has been published, we normally have no clue about what the initial draft looked like and what changes were demanded by reviewers. While there may be good reasons for guaranteeing the anonymity of reviewers, making the different drafts and rounds of comments digitally available would allow for more transparency and—through the force of social embarrassment—counteract the tendency among authors to exceedingly adjust to the, sometimes, shattering demands of reviewers. This may encourage fewer texts being published, which is a good side effect, and it would also allow for (anonymous) reviews of reviewers (cf. Baxt et al., 1998), and lead to debate on how a good reviewer should behave. Currently, there is scant evidence that peer review increases the quality of published articles (Couzin-Frankel, 2013), although few people doubt that many poor papers are justifiably rejected. Unless the point of reviews is simply to promote authors who have the most endurance and willingness to compromise, we should use every means necessary to make this process more than a meaningless ritual.[1]

Another institutional reform that is even more modest in terms of openness is to make publicly funded research open to the public—that is, *open access*. Most members of the public do not have the resources to pay $32 or even more for reading a scientific article. The research remains locked up in journals to which only those with accounts at university libraries have access. This represents a scam of grotesque proportions: publicly funded universities are forced to buy publicly funded research from private publishers. With the Internet radically reducing overhead costs for printing and distribution, there is no longer any rational reason for accepting the fees demanded by publishers. Today, all four major scientific publishers (Springer, Wiley, Informa, and Elsevier) consistently report profits that exceed a third of all revenue (Taylor, 2012).

The perversion of this market is not restricted to the publication of articles. As an anonymous researcher in the *Guardian* recently testified, academics are

---

[1] There is a risk that time and effort is put into making everything accessible, without much coming out of this. As there are complaints about limited interest in published papers, there may be less interest in following the often lengthy process from first submission to reviews and resubmissions and so forth, of published papers. People interested in one or a few cases can always contact the author and ask for copies of the material. Still, it should be noted that these processes could easily be automized.

being hoodwinked into writing books nobody can buy. Even reasonably reputable publishers will occasionally contact researchers to ask them to write books that will only be published in hardback for £60 to £150 and sometimes beyond. Needless to say, few individuals will ever buy these books, but some university libraries may. This is not a market that has been established to allow for specialist literature that otherwise would never be published. The costs for publishing a book has been drastically reduced in recent years, and since publishers do not pay the researchers' salaries, their expenses are very small. What we see is rather an exploitation of academics and public resources that could easily be stopped if academics collectively boycotted publishers in this business. As the anonymous researcher in the *Guardian* puts it:

> We could stop publishing these books altogether—which may be advisable in a time of hysterical mass publication. Or we publish only with decent publishers, who believe that books are meant to be read and not simply profited from. And if it's only a matter of making research available, then of course there's open source publishing, which most academics are aware of by now.   (Anonymous, 2015b)

Even if such open source publishing is currently less prestigious and often suffers from low or at least uncertain quality, it offers some opportunities to disseminate work to wider audiences. However, the risk of disseminating less meaningful and low-quality work is huge. We need quality filters and these are costly. As we emphasize throughout this book, the age of mass research and mass publication has led to a perverse relationship between authors wanting to write and publish, and a shortage of readers. As this is a key aspect of meaninglessness in research, quality control is vital. And publishers are vital here; even though some fail to use clear quality standards, there are many publishers that are selective about what they publish and try to ensure quality control, and are thus likely to offer readers something worth reading. If we push for some downplaying of journal articles and encouragement to write high-quality, more broadly accessible books, then we also need to nurture the ideal of the responsible, quality-assuring academic publisher, and push for the reduction of greediness of publishers.

Promoting Meaningful Research at University and Departmental Levels

Downgrading Instrumentalism Associated with Careerism

Academic careers and the thirst for promotion is probably the single most potent driver behind the proliferation of research publications and the omnipotence of the academic publishing game that we have criticized in this book. The rise of unbridled careerism in academia is a relatively recent phenomenon, at least in many European countries and also Australia. Until the 1990s, the promotion of academics was a less salient issue. In the UK, most academics worked as lecturers or senior lecturers and occasionally a chair was advertised and people applied for this. Most departments in social science had one or only a small handful of professors. Promotion to chairs or even readerships was rare and not foremost in the minds of most academics. To end one's career as a lecturer or a senior lecturer was no cause for embarrassment and in no way indicated a failed or derailed career.

Now all this has changed. Many countries have entered an era of academic hyper-promotion. This may vary across different countries and disciplines but, with very few exceptions, academics expect promotion and the eagerness for getting a better title is strong. Regularly we see the promotion of people with modest merits which fuels the appetite of others and intensifies rivalries and envy. Promotion is often less about competence and contribution than a reward for a number of publications, often multi-authored, that boost an institution's ranking. Researchers with publications in top-ranked journals are often attracted to new jobs with the promise of enhanced titles, conditions of work, and salaries in a situation that begins to resemble the football transfer market. The movement of academics across institutions, especially in the UK, has increased dramatically. This has paradoxically led both to a significant devaluation of titles, especially that of professor, and an increased hunger for it among those who do not possess it.

Over-promotion is both an outcome of and a driver of careerism. With promotion possibilities there is a strong focus on climbing up the greasy pole towards better and better titles with the privileges and rewards that follow. This can of course be seen as democratic and fair—the elitism of a system with few and rare promotions and a limited number of senior academics is not unproblematic. But in the context of meaningless research, the effects of over-promotion are undeniably contributing to the problem. We are in an age of promotion-driven research. Careerism—based on 'mechanical' recognition and title-climbing rather than respect for important scholarly contributions—is a major ill.

We make two proposals. The first is to *reduce the incentive structure* and counteract narrow careerism associated with over-promotion. We actually believe that stopping internal promotion entirely would be a good idea. We have seen that academic careerism has been a root cause of the proliferation of meaningless outputs in social research and a corresponding devaluation of teaching and scholarship. We believe that a senior title should come as a confirmation of competence and not be seen as the main target in itself. To this end, we would propose that criteria for promotion, if used, or the attainment of associate or full professorship, should be much broader and harder to achieve. Application in an open competition for a senior position would counteract instrumentalist efforts to meet minimalistic criteria for internal promotion. Being a co-author of a number of articles, even in highly-ranked journals, and being 'acceptable' as a teacher and administrator would not by itself qualify for promotion. This may be seen as intolerable to the title-hungry young academic, but the 'title satisfaction' of a university lecturer twenty-five years ago was probably equivalent to that of an associate professor today. Titles and promotion are part of a zero-sum game—it is the relative position in relation to others that matters. The more individuals are promoted to the rank of professor, the lesser the value of the title, the lesser the satisfaction it affords to those who have it, and the greater its allure to those who do not have it. The frustration of being a 'mere' lecturer or associate professor increases correspondingly. So the fixation on formal titles (and associated privileges) is understandable from an individual's short-term point of view, but does not really add much to the long-term satisfaction of a collective. Individuals are drawn into career instrumentalism for fear of falling behind and partly as a response to the fallen status of the higher education sector as a whole. As said, it is a zero-sum game. And it is well known that an emphasis on instrumental rewards tends to reduce intrinsic motivation and work satisfaction (Salancik & Pfeffer 1978). Inherently satisfying features of the work are downplayed as extrinsic motivation takes over an individual's outlook.

To this end, we propose to *sharpen and broaden* the criteria for promotion, tenure, and hiring. Instead of primarily counting numbers of publications and the kudos of the journals in which they feature, decisions on hiring, tenure, and promotion can encompass a much wider range of considerations. These include the following:

- The social relevance of the journal articles under consideration as well as an ability to produce at least some high-quality solo publications.
- Other types of publications (including books and book chapters) and their social value and meaning.
- A high general level of broader scholarship as ascertained by innumerable indicators, including book reviews, editorial contributions, conference organizing, successful doctoral supervision and examining, international collaborations and funding, recognition by extra-academic bodies.
- A serious revaluation of teaching as a central aspect to scholarship, including testimonials from students, innovative teaching practices, textbook and pedagogical publications, and properly administered teaching evaluations, including peer-reviewed lectures.

We recognize that diluting the emphasis on journal publication as the dominant criterion for career building carries the risk of arbitrary and politically motivated decisions. It can also lower the bar and open up for endless hopes and expectations of promotions. Assessments and rewards can become a matter of social connections and nepotism. Social relevance, teaching, and general scholarship are hard to assess. The risk of power abuses is obvious if peer reviews are substituted by boss rule or committees engaged in deals and compromises. It is also difficult to say 'no' to people if 'everything' counts. An emphasis on meaningful research needs to focus on strong and unique research contributions of social relevance and value. To this end, we do not question the importance of peer-reviewed publications or indeed citation metrics which are relatively objective and do not necessarily privilege particular types of outputs. An advantage of citation metrics is that they are fairly format-neutral—a good book or an innovative article in a lesser journal may score higher than a mundane 'contribution' in a star journal. We will come back to the pros and cons of citations and how these can be used in thoughtful ways when discussing our proposals at the policy level in Chapter 8.

In making promotion, tenure, and appointment decisions, university departments can also discourage extreme specialization and strong emphasis on the quantity of publications. Publications in which there is more than 50 per cent overlap should be discounted. More importantly, however, it is the value and social meaning of the publications that should count rather than the number of items on long lists. Research should not be the dominant or only criterion in such decisions. As we have argued throughout this book, teaching and citizenship are vital aspects of being a scholar and there have to be cases of outstanding contributions in these areas that merit clear recognition. Scholars who have dedicated a lifetime to educating the younger generations and who have tirelessly given their time and energy enhancing the quality of life in their departments should not be seen as second-class citizens, hitting various glass ceilings that are easily sidestepped by their peers whose main preoccupation is with hits in top journals.

We believe that these measures would discourage some of the worst excesses and injustices that afflict academic careers and which, in the view of some, are more directly felt by women and members of minority groups. Over the years, there have been claims that the institutional obstacles bar the path of women scholars from reaching the highest echelons of academic ladders. Some argue that both the publications-driven promotion and many of the types of research and writing favoured by social science journals systematically disadvantage women scholars and minority groups (for example, Berger, Benschop, & van den Brink, 2015; Fotaki, 2013; Phillips, & and Rhodes, 2014). Shaking up the criteria for promotion, tenure, and appointment along the lines outlined above could have a beneficial effect on the careers of women and minority groups who, for a variety of rehearsed reasons, may be currently disadvantaged by the publishing game. This is not to deny that the double blind peer review promotes a degree of meritocracy.

Against (Bureaucratic) Research Ethics

A strong deterrent to meaningful research is formulaic research ethics. There is much variation between countries and even universities. Different disciplines, but even more so research topics, vary widely in the constraints and influences exercised as research ethics. Often an emphasis on formal research ethics, with committees, procedures, and constraints, directly pushes research into less relevance and significance. Research easily becomes cautious and uncritical. Informed consent may make interviewees constrained in what they say and make some experiments impossible to carry out. Flexible research which violates pre-agreed protocols or methodologies by seizing unexpected, emerging possibilities are deterred.

One of the most significant set of studies ever carried out in social science is Milgram's (1974) work on authority and obedience. This showed an extreme degree of inclination to mindlessly follow what was thought to be legitimate authority among average US citizens. The results are worrying, thought-provoking, and score as high as they can get in terms of meaningful research. Today, research ethics conventions in most academic institutions would most likely prevent this type of research.

A recent alarming example is from the University of Queensland, Brisbane. Here a study observed a number of students of different backgrounds getting on buses pretending their pay cards had run out of money. The study's authors found that drivers allowed white and east Asian passengers to ride free about 72 per cent of the time, but only 50 per cent for Indian and 36 per cent for black passengers. The evidence of racial discrimination was unambiguous. Rather than celebrating this socially meaningful type of research that could lead to practical improvements, university top management tried hard to censure the responsible professor, first through demotion (from full to assistant professor) and then through a warning for misconduct. Apparently the 'victims' of the study, the bus company and the drivers, should have been informed of the study and informed consent been given (*Guardian*, 26 February 2015). This would, obviously, have made the research impossible.

There are of course areas of research involving vulnerable groups where formal ethics procedures are essential. Often formal ethics lead to people ticking off the boxes and minimizing using their full judgement, which easily leads to a boomerang effect in terms of the ethical consequences. As a distinguished professor of public health in Great Britain put it to one of the authors: 'were we to be honest about our research to the Research Ethics Committees, they would place restrictions on our practice that would make our work as researchers less ethical'. Universities, research foundations, and professional associations need to be very careful in imposing strict, formal, ethical standards and procedures if meaning in research is to be reclaimed.

Training and Workshops

Schools and departments could also reduce the dominance of incremental gap-spotting research by nurturing a more reflective scholarly orientation and consensus-challenging research through *training and workshops*. For example, instead of mainly cultivating academics as paper authors for journals, more training and workshops on questioning assumptions, creative writing, writing for a broader audience, and encouragement of research book publications are needed. Needless to say, we are not arguing against journal publications—they are a key quality improvement and assurance resource tool and major outlet for research—but to vary intellectual work and give space for contributions makes it more difficult to shoehorn work into the contemporary standard journal format. As all academics are so exposed to journal publications, and because these tend to be so standardized, there is actually limited need for workshops improving their skills. Simple imitation is possible. Writing for a broader audience, for example, academics and (educated) others seriously interested in a topic, is harder, calls for more imagination and ability to write well and in varied ways, and could be crucial to support. Here one could do a distinction between 'pure' popularization—writing for a layman audience wanting infotainment—and writing in a more accessible and engaging way for an academic and educated public audience prepared to read somewhat more demanding texts. Our key concern in this book is the latter, with for example Fromm (1941, 1976), Klein (2000), Sennett (1998, 2006), Foley (2010), Kunda (1992), and Burenstam Linder (1969) as exemplars. Our interest in this book, as we hope to have made clear, is social science research and how to make it more meaningful. We are not primarily targeting science journalism or 'pure' popularization—even if the boundaries between different genres are not always clear.

Creative and engaging writing workshops could target, for example, how to make journal articles less formulaic and boring, or how to write books that have a broader appeal than a pure intra-academic or textbook market. This is badly in need of support. With Michael Billig (2013) we could suggest the slogan for workshops and courses: 'Writing Less Badly'. Or 'Writing Not for Journal Publication'.

Education and PhD Training

In order for academics to do meaningful research rather than seek return on their investment, they must be socialized to this type of work from an early age through texts, seminars, and lectures that encourage a more reflective orientation. Questions on the meaning and social value of social research should occupy as much or more time than discussions on method, theory, and data analysis—which is not to say that these themes are not unimportant. A difficulty here is that social value easily leads to broad—and maybe too broad—questions with no clear answers. How to increase innovation, how to improve health, how to reduce discrimination, to help a municipality improve public services are very vital issues, but ones that do not permit easy answers and tend to be too broad for a research project.

Only a small minority of all students will be pursuing a PhD or a research career. Ideally, however, all graduates moving into professional or other qualified jobs will benefit from an active reflection on questions of meaning and not only within their narrow field of expertise. A more holistic orientation on how to deal with issues in working life (including conflicts, abuses of power, discrimination, disagreements, group tensions, and so forth) calls for learning to think in reflective and creative ways. Here research and education that work in tandem would be very important. It calls for mutual support of teaching and research that challenge the McDonaldization of higher education (Ritzer, 2004), one in which students are not consumers of knowledge but active participants and co-creators (Naidoo & Williams, 2015). By contrast, increasing specialization and standardization of research around tacit formulas, coupled with an increasing emphasis on 'textbook learning', separates inquiry from learning and decouples instead of integrating the core practices of scholarship. The outcome is a loss of meaning for social research.

The socialization of PhD students is absolutely crucial for the recovery of meaning in social research. Unfortunately, current doctoral training programmes in many countries and disciplines seem tailor-made to encourage formulaic, technically competent, and substantially meaningless research. PhD students typically mimic the research ideals of their supervisors and significant others. What these people do, more than what they preach, helps shape the students' outlooks and their subsequent careers. Currently the role models for most of these students are star-academics with many journal 'hits' and regular cites, and the models of publication they seek to emulate in their own work are highly specialized, technical, and often largely meaningless articles. A shift in emphasis to more meaningful research would inevitably call for substantial changes in PhD training and socialization.

A first thing to recognize is that a PhD, central as it is to a researcher's life story, is different from subsequent research. This is partly due to the vulnerability and dependence of young scholars seeking to build their professional identities. Much of the work involved in writing a thesis is training. The thesis itself is more a matter of meaning for the student—the learning and qualification developed and demonstrated—than for the rest of the world. But if the years of PhD study do not lead to at least some genuinely exciting findings and arguments one can question if they are worth the effort. Some meaning beyond the purely individual one for the PhD students needs to be asked for. The central principles of a PhD should emphasize the broader relevance of research, and at least avoid socializing the PhD into what is now normal social science. Broader scholarship, non-formulaic research and writing, and some risk-taking are necessary even if this means that a larger proportion of those starting a PhD will not finish, at least not in the scheduled time, and sometimes not at all. This may mean tragedies for the poor PhD students, but the idea of social science and PhDs cannot be to adapt the level so that the standard is mediocre and we cultivate academics with a poor sense of scholarship.

A disturbing feature of many contemporary PhD programmes is the inclination to accept too many students. This is especially the case in countries where student fees play an important role in university finances and/or the presence of numerous doctoral students is seen as a sign of research excellence. Quantity is generally earned at the expense of quality. Another disturbing feature is the increased tendency to structure PhD programmes so that they maximize the PhD students' visible indicators of employability. This has led to many universities supplanting the doctorate by thesis with doctorates by academic publications, where candidates are typically required to demonstrate that they have prepared three or four publishable or just-worthy-of-review papers in reputable journals. This generally has negative consequences, as doctoral candidates are socialized into the publishing game before they can establish their credentials as scholars with a rounded grounding, and so they come to view this game as the core activity of an academic career. In some countries, papers acceptable towards doctorates may be co-authored with the students' supervisors and others. This further undermines the students' ability to develop their own voice, socializing them instead to the messy dynamics of co-authorship, journal submissions, anonymous reviews, and the like.

We are firmly opposed to this trend, and seek to vindicate afresh the meaning of the social science doctorate as a once-in-a-lifetime opportunity for young scholars to demonstrate that they have mastered their disciplines in breadth and depth, that they have developed their skills as empirical researchers, that they are able to communicate their arguments in a scholarly manner to a wider audience and, above all, that they can undertake original and socially relevant inquiry.

In Conclusion

In this chapter, we have made some proposals that will encourage more innovative and influential research by *countering narrow instrumentalism* at the institutional level. We have advocated less rapid and less frequent promotion by reducing title inflation and reliance on journal publications, and using broader criteria for employment, tenure, and promotion that reflect individuals' contributions as researchers, teachers, *and* citizens in their academic institutions. All this will encourage the development of scholars—well-read, reflective academics—rather than journal publication technicians. For social science scholars, books are a natural publication outlet. We strongly warn against attitudes and communications like one from a professor who said that 'I wouldn't advise anyone to write a book—it's career suicide' (cited in Clarke & Knights 2015, p. 1873). This instrumentalist view is common, and partly responsible for the sad state of affairs. We have also made proposals on doctoral training and other institutional arrangements—workshops, ethics procedures—that will enhance a move away from instrumental, constrained, and bureaucratic research. We have highlighted the need for training programmes that, instead of employability, stress creativity, risk-taking, and space for variation to increase the likelihood of meaning-oriented researchers. In place of writing and publishing workshops and courses, we advocate write-invitingly workshops. As we argued in the Introduction to this book, the value of research is tied to members of society being able to read and understand social science texts and being engaged with them in both their thinking and their practice.

8

Recovering Meaning Through Policy Changes

In the previous chapters we made some recommendations aimed at recovering meaning in social science research on two levels: individual academics, and academic institutions. Beyond these levels, there are wider structural forces shaping higher education and academic research that cannot be ignored when discussing the conditions for a return to meaning. In recent years, higher education has been increasingly brought under the remit of a neo-liberal agenda emphasizing competition, markets, and choice; it has become increasingly global in as much as labour markets for academic work have opened up under the increasing hegemony of the English language as the lingua franca of research; it has been deeply affected by new social and technological developments affecting the production, publishing, and dissemination of knowledge; and, as we noted earlier, it has turned from an elite to a mass industry. There are frequent reports that the labour market for academics has become ever more precarious (cf. Bourdieu, 1998; Standing, 2011) and the conditions of work ever more pressurized. Even though there are reasons to be somewhat cautious about alarmist reports, there seems to be a clear change in the way higher education is organized and funded in many parts of the world. In the 1970s, temporary appointments in American colleges and universities were practically unheard of, whereas three decades later so-called fixed-term, non-tenure track appointments are the basis for the majority of full-time appointments (Schuster & Finkelstein, 2008, p. 356). Against this backcloth of mass education and increasing precarization, an increasing number of academics become eager to secure a safe position for themselves. Many are also eager to get employment and advance their careers as researchers in the more prestigious higher education institutions, in a sector that is highly diverse, and in which not every institution can claim to be a member of the elite.

This is an example of how some of the problems we have described in this book stem from structural forces beyond the organization of universities. Another example is the pressure to demonstrate the economic value of research to the rest of society. As higher education becomes part of the so-called knowledge society and an ever-larger part of the economy, national governments increasingly see it as their responsibility to regulate the sector, primarily through different funding and regulatory mechanisms. With the expansion of higher education and a growing army of academics, there is an increased concern to demonstrate that something valuable—apart from the self-actualization and career ambitions of academics—comes out of the public spending. Government investment in research and higher education is widely regarded as supporting the growth of innovation, the rise of new services and commodities, new companies, and job creation. Different countries adopt different policies, often contradictory or inconsistent, which reflect the outcomes of political debates, compromises, and conflicts. For many business schools in Anglo-Saxon countries the recruitment of overseas students is central, as they cross-subsidize less popular and poorer disciplines. Sometimes business schools are more business than schools.

Among critical scholars, resisting this instrumentalization of research has been an important issue dating back at least a century. During the 1960s, for instance, the Frankfurt philosopher Herbert Marcuse argued that the academy should constitute an enclave of thinking and criticism free from extra-academic considerations, political or economic. As Ronald Reagan, then governor of California, ran a campaign to have Marcuse dismissed from the faculty, he personally felt the fragility of academic freedom (Marcuse, 2005). The need to continuously defend this freedom was recently restated by English Professor Thomas Docherty in *Universities at War*. As he succinctly describes, we now see a clash between those who see the university as a servant of national economic interests, and those who emphasize its emancipatory capacity to extend social justice, freedom, and democracy. As Docherty sees it, the latter are currently losing:

> Just as governments increasingly serve the 1%, so also university governance serves the whim or will of the President, VC, CEO and their central team. Do they care about the university? Do they care about free speech? Increasingly, the answer is obvious, clear and quite undoubtedly shocking: No.   (Docherty, 2014, p. 140)

This critique is not only concerned with the lack of meaningful research, but also with the need for critically engaged research embracing emancipatory values. Acknowledging the structural forces forming universities and other organizations, it reminds us that the university can never become an island of conviviality cut off from the society surrounding it. Hence, policy suggestions are always ideological in the sense that they, sometimes unwittingly, take the present conditions for granted. Recognizing this quandary, we here offer some recommendations for governmental policies that we believe will help researchers, in particular social scientists, to focus their inquiries on work of social value and meaning. We address the issues of rankings and assessments, of metrics aimed at evaluating social impact and community engagement, and indicate ways of countering rampant instrumentalism and careerism among researchers.

Higher Education Policies

Academics themselves do not like government attempts to regulate their work, or centralized initiatives aimed at monitoring and evaluating the quality of their outputs. Many will find compelling Berg and Seeber's idea of the 'slow professor' who steps out of the treadmill and takes time to read, reflect, talk with colleagues, and write slowly while mindfully resisting the corporatization and the 'culture of speed' in the academy. But how can this ethical ideal turn into a policy proposition within the frames of neo-liberal capitalism? As Berg and Seeber repeatedly recognize, 'you can't put a good conversation on your vitae' (2016, p. 85). Relaxing the continual assessments, giving researchers more time to think and to converse in corridors, and using purely qualitative judgements as the basis for distributing limited resources may create a more convivial environment for those who are already in academic jobs, but leisurely conversations do not guarantee meaningful social knowledge. Such a system would also be more liable to arbitrariness and nepotism. Scholars who advocate the need for 'relaxation' cannot simply wish away the competition, exclusion, and discrimination inherent in the economic and political structures which modern universities inhabit. In these structures where governments bear a substantial burden of funding research, there are legitimate concerns that public resources should be used wisely and efficiently.

Knowledge generated through public funds must be accessible to others who may assess its meaning and value and make use of it for the public good. For this reason, we oppose the blanket removal of all research evaluation schemes. We also do not believe, somewhat against prevalent views, that ever greater government funding for university research with no further regulation and monitoring would resolve the problems we have identified in this book. Actually, as we pointed out earlier, part of the problem is the sheer quantity of research, and the last thing we need is more publications. Resources parcelled out by governments to universities have to be assessed against other social claims, and a degree of government control over the spending of these resources is necessary. Governments should not dictate how research funds are spent, but they do have an overall responsibility to make sure that public funds and student fees are not wasted. We need to recognize that academics and their institutions have wider social responsibilities and that no government, not even the most neo-liberal one, can give them a free rein to do as they please. Governments often make mistakes and higher education policies, like all policies, are liable to prove ineffective or counterproductive. In democratic countries, electorates have a chance, if only every few years, to judge how well public policies represent their values and their interests, and to make their views known through their vote. Politicians and higher education policy-makers are faced with many difficult questions like:

- How much control over higher education should be exercised centrally and how much can be achieved at the policy level?
- How should the funding be distributed across universities, faculties, disciplines, sectors, and departments?
- How should the products of research be evaluated and how should these evaluations influence future funding decisions?
- What proportions of funding should come directly from government as against funding from external research agencies?
- How should higher education funding be split between research and teaching?
- How widely should research foundations and agencies spread their funding?
- Should research grants be allocated on the basis of peer evaluations or should external stakeholders also be consulted?
- Should large grants go to 'tried and tested' senior researchers or should they go to younger and potentially more adventurous and innovative ones?
- What proportions of funding should go to applied and practical research with immediate potential applications compared to more academically defined projects?
- Should funding privilege high-risk endeavours or reliable, middle-of-the-road projects?

These are important and difficult questions indicating some of the complexities facing higher education policy-makers. Our own general position is that, given the widespread dissatisfaction with the social contributions of social science we discussed in Part 1, it is wise not to spread resources too thinly across or inside institutions. This inevitably means that resources in many institutions will be better spent on teaching rather than research, and also that in many institutions research resources (budgets, time, and so forth) will not be distributed evenly across departments and faculty. At the risk of being dismissed as nostalgic or elitist, we believe that there is merit in not all institutions and all academics aspiring for research excellence which, as we have seen, leads to fetishizing of the publishing game and all the resulting quandaries. Concentration and specialization do not mean that social science research should become the preserve of a few faculty members in elite universities and even fewer star-researchers in other places. But it would probably be a good thing if public resources for research are not distributed on an equal basis across all institutions, concentrating instead on those institutions that can demonstrate sustained excellence in high-quality and socially relevant research. Some form of evaluation of research is, therefore, inevitable and desirable and it is better that this should be undertaken by government bodies (with extensive participation of academics themselves) rather than commercial interests keen to create rankings and lists.

A key challenge in this context is to identify measures that establish impartial, transparent, and relatively robust assessments, involving both expert judgements and quantitative indicators, to determine the value of social research in different institutions and then to devise a system for allocating resources accordingly. This has been the aim of various Research Assessment Evaluation (RAE) and Research Excellence Framework (REF) schemes in the UK and Australia. These schemes rely on appointed panels of peers to investigate and evaluate four publications per research-active faculty member over a period of five or six years, intended to give an overall picture of the research quality of each department. A variety of rankings are then compiled, ostensibly reflecting the research status of each university department. The effects of these schemes which were first introduced twenty-five or so years ago have been extensive and contradictory. Some of their consequences are direct and unambiguous. They have hugely increased competition among universities, many of which now view their position in the rankings as a matter of life or death. They have greatly enhanced the status and privileges of researchers with starred publications. These researchers can now command very high salaries, and regularly move from institution to institution on the strength of their publications, which can substantially raise a department's position in the rankings. They have, thus, intensified inequalities among academics, with those seen as ineligible to be 'submitted' for the purposes of evaluation usually ending up with increased teaching and administrative loads. They have beyond any doubt confirmed research as a superior activity to teaching, one on which academic careers crucially depend, and, relatedly, have led to the ballooning of academic publications and journals of dubious quality that we have castigated in this book.

Predictably, many university departments have approached these research evaluations as an effective means to monitor, assess, and discipline the performance of individual researchers, elevating the publishing game to an end in its own right. This involves the classic conundrum of displacement from ends (good research across a department) to means (individuals publishing in prestigious journals or, failing this, in less prestigious ones). The wish to climb in the rankings has led to the dominance of safe, narrow, instrumental, ultra-specialized, and formulaic research and its corollary, a cottage industry criticizing and bemoaning the hegemony of journal rankings and lists.

While sharing and even instigating many of the criticisms levelled at existing research evaluation schemes, we do not advocate their abolition. Instead we propose their far-reaching reform based on three proposals:

(a) A streamlined and flexible scheme for assessing a *limited number of key research contributions* from each department. This should be sensitive to the unique qualities of research in different disciplines and fields of social science.

(b) A sensitive and nuanced interpretation and evaluation of *bibliometrics*, including citation statistics.

(c) The use of metrics to generate a more rounded and discipline-relevant assessment of the *social value and relevance* of research. This should include criteria regarding the dissemination, use, and impact of research across different audiences, including non-academic ones.

Before expanding on these proposals, let us briefly comment on the cost, thoroughness, and legitimacy of research evaluations. The cost of a thorough research evaluation scheme is high. Lord Stern's (2016) review of the 2014 REF in the UK estimated that the cost of the evaluation was just under £5,000 for each of the 50,000 academics evaluated. Nearly twice as many academics were left out of the evaluation, presumably because their research was not seen to be of sufficiently good quality and its inclusion would 'drag down' the position of their department in the rankings. More than 1,000 eminent scholars made up the panels which carried out the evaluations, and each one of these academics spent virtually an entire year on this process. Clearly, the involvement of so many distinguished academics in the evaluation increased its cost but its legitimacy too—in spite of many criticisms of the REF, its fundamental legitimacy has not been called into question, either by those who did well out of it or by those who did not. In spite of the criticisms noted above, the REF and similar schemes have been accepted with minimal resistance from academics themselves across the sector.

Any assessment system needs to balance cost and legitimacy. Inexpensive assessments are simplistic and mechanical. They encourage sub-optimization, their legitimacy is limited and they can be entirely counterproductive. Systems that seek to do justice to quality with highly elaborate procedures can be very costly and labour intensive. Having a large group of experts reading vast numbers of outputs and trying to compare their value is costly and often inaccurate. We therefore need to develop systems that are sensitive to quality without involving enormous efforts and complexity. For this reason, journal publications and citation counts can hardly be avoided. Peer reviews and citations generally reflect the judgements of fellow academics. They are less sensitive to capricious opinions, biased judgements, local conventions and preferences, and nepotism. The expert opinions of evaluation panels, whose members have their own likes and dislikes, specialisms and blind spots, must be balanced with some more impersonal criteria, like the ability to generate research funds and to earn citations from other scholars. In every case, however, both subjective evaluations and quantitative indicators must be used with great care.

Broad Assessments of Key Contributions

Instead of assessing large numbers of publications from numerous researchers, we favour an evaluation of a relatively small number of key research contributions per department. Thus, instead of counting every article in which a researcher's name features, often amidst numerous others from many different institutions, we would require social science departments or schools to single out their most outstanding contributions, based on a combination of scientific value and social significance over a time period. Depending on the size of a department or school, a relatively limited number of contributions (possibly fewer than twenty even for large departments) could be selected for evaluation. Truly significant contributions would include outstanding journal articles which become landmarks for subsequent debates. They would also include books, reports, and other writings addressed to a broader public, as well as influential policy reports that are judged as innovative in addressing pressing social issues and needs. In the case of contributions of exceptional value and quality, unpublished texts like book or paper manuscripts could be submitted for assessment. Nominated contributions will need to be carefully evaluated, by panels of academic experts, but also other individuals of sound judgement who can take a broader view, for example academics from other disciplines, respected journalists, public intellectuals, and academically interested professionals. One could even imagine a form of blind review where all texts are sent in their final manuscript form, so that indications of the publication outlet are removed, as far as possible. Evaluators would then be forced to evaluate an academic contribution on its own qualities rather than the prestige of the publication in which it is published. Evaluations should address the quality of the outputs in relation to the resources available for the research. Different departments in each field may then be compared and ranked or grouped in line with their contributions relative to the funding they receive. The allocation of governmental resources could then be partly contingent on these evaluations to encourage universities and departments to consider seriously what is vital, and what makes a difference, and move away from a one-sided emphasis on quantity and the bean-counting of articles in top journals.

We realize that this would be a difficult and potentially conflict-laden task at the local level. Criteria should be flexible and even vague. This would lead to some decision anxiety, but would also generate productive discussions within institutions which restores the question of social meaning on the agenda. What is the broader social value of what we are aiming to accomplish? How much of the millions we spend every year on funding research is of true scientific *and* social value? Which of the hundreds of research papers and books claimed by our faculty are worth highlighting as clear contributions to humankind and not just as clever or less clever variations of what has been said already? Prompting such discussions and creating an awareness would strongly support a focus on meaning in communication, in research priorities, and in the identity constructions of researchers.

Cautious Use of Bibliometrics

As noted in the earlier section, the primary way in which existing schemes seek to evaluate research quality and influence is mostly through rating articles in A-listed journals over a specific period. This is marred with difficulties and strongly encourages incremental, highly specialized, and generally meaningless research. An examination of the citation statistics of individual articles demonstrates a weak relation to the prestige of the journal in which they are published (Adler & Harzing, 2009). As Pfeffer (2007, p. 1342) noted, research on citation counts 'illustrates that a shockingly high proportion of papers, even those published in elite journals, garner *zero* citations, with an even larger percentage obtaining very few'. A careful and critical consideration of *citation counts* of different contributions, rather than the presumed quality of the journals in which they are published, could be a more appropriate indicator of quality.

Using citation counts as a performance indicator has, needless to say, its own problems (Adler & Harzing, 2009; Grey, 2010). There are many exclusive clubs of authors who mainly cite each other, and rarely cite authors outside their specific club (Macdonald and Kam, 2010). Writings on fashionable topics may get an undeserved amount of attention. It can take a few years before it is possible to judge the extent to which an article is cited. Methodology and review papers tend to get cited more than theoretical and empirical studies. Self-citations may further bias citation statistics although most databases can now eliminate this bias. For all these reasons, it is crucial to avoid simplistic metrics. Method textbooks and multiple co-authorship need to be considered, perhaps removing scores from pure textbooks and dividing points by the number of authors contributing to each publication. The age of researchers also needs to be considered, since older researchers inevitably attract more citations. Finally, and perhaps most importantly, a difference must be drawn between articles routinely cited in strings of publications ostensibly supporting a certain argument, and those with which other researchers engage actively to develop their own ideas. In spite of these difficulties, qualitatively moderated and 'cleansed' citation counts can give an indication of whether particular researchers are read by scholars or not. This would stimulate stronger efforts to produce innovative and influential studies, even if the sheer volume of publications decreased. Carefully used, citations say something about what is viewed as interesting and significant. They also demonstrate whether someone's work is read only by a few members of a microtribe and ritualistically cited by them, or whether it reaches a wider community of scholars and a broader range of disciplines in social science. Special credit can be given to publications that cross disciplinary boundaries and are cited in journals of different fields, something that would encourage inter-disciplinary scholarship.

We realize that every indicator of research quality is imperfect and potentially unfair. The same applies to bibliometrics. There are anomalies: many articles are routinely referenced without being read and, conversely, some hidden gems may linger unnoticed and uncited. This, however, does not rule out the potential uses of carefully processed citation statistics as one of several indicators of research quality. A strong movement to enhance the meaning of social research needs to highlight what is regarded as valuable and relevant, both by the academic and other communities. It is unlikely that citations aggregated over an entire department will be glaringly inaccurate or unfair. Most of us frequently cite publications we find impressive. And of course we are not advocating citation counts at the expense of other criteria of high-quality social research that is not properly reflected in citations. We do, however, believe that it is perverse to ignore citations as one of the criteria that can help the evaluation of research quality.

An advantage of citations is that they facilitate assessment of a *broader range of publication formats*. Instead of relying exclusively on designated journal lists, other types of publication are regularly cited and can be included as high-quality research. These include books and book chapters, practitioner-oriented journals and magazines, reports to governments and NGOs, and online materials. Indeed many respected scholars receive more citations from such publications than from those in peer-reviewed journals. Overall, therefore, we believe that, given the current state of overproduction of research publications, some impersonal quantitative indicators like citation counts can offer at least a complementary picture of the merits of different research contributions and can play a useful role in the assessment of institutions. They are, of course, also routinely used in appointments, tenure, and promotion decisions for individual academics.

The Impact of Academic Research on Academic, Professional, and Public Audiences

Our third proposal to encourage meaningful research concerns an evaluation of the impact of academic research and its reach and influence outside academia. The measurement of impact has, in recent years, become a considerable concern of governments and agencies seeking to evaluate the quality of academic research. In the UK, the 2014 Research Excellence Framework included a measure for impact that accounted for 20 per cent of the marks awarded to each institution. This proved particularly difficult to operationalize and was not popular with academics or institutions. 'Impact' quickly became a box-ticking exercise—a highly mechanistic but time-consuming device ostensibly to demonstrate that academics do not inhabit ivory towers doing irrelevant work. It encouraged a tissue of fabrications, hypes, and lies where the most spurious connections were made in order to tick the boxes and claim relevance for dubious academic work. These included letters from managers and professionals claiming to have benefited from various half-baked innovations emanating from university departments. Impact was used indiscriminately across disciplines like medicine, engineering, astrophysics, and humanities, as if all these domains of knowledge contribute to society in the same way. For academics in Management and Business Schools 'impact' was frequently equated with anything that is of use to business and profit, mostly as part of a neo-liberal agenda.

In spite of such a potential for abuse, we believe that in addition to assessing the quality of different publications discussed above, some measurement of their social impact and relevance is necessary. Like panel evaluations and citation metrics, measures of impact and relevance must be applied with circumspection to avoid gaming and hyped up claims. Three types of impact may usefully be distinguished.

- *Academic impact* reflected in citations in academic outlets and obtainable from Google Scholar, SSCI/Thompson and other databases.

- *Public impact* reflected in attention from the mass and social media. This involves citations in newspapers, popular journals, broadcasts, and so forth as well as hits and 'likes' in social media. Public impact is also made through expert opinions offered to press, broadcast, and electronic media that reach broader audiences

- *Expert impact* on professional and public bodies, through specifically commissioned reports and articles, participation in boards and committees, talks to professional associations, and other types of expert work.

The first type of impact was discussed earlier, so we will now limit ourselves to the other two. Public impact is easiest indicated by citations in the mass media and, increasingly, the social media. A problem here is that some academics are eager to appear in the media and comment on almost everything, even if their claims carry little weight. Media coverage can also be based on negative reasons, for example, making an unwise statement or creating a scandal. All the same, metrics on media coverage can be cleansed to indicate the extent to which different academics have the willingness and the capacity to reach broader audiences.

Currently, a number of universities are realizing the power of social media in bringing their research to wider audiences. Several online platforms have been established to this end, like the Huffington Post, the Conversation, and Open-Democracy, publishing online shorter articles by academics seeking to bring their research to broader audiences in more accessible forms. Some of these platforms, like the Conversation, employ qualified journalists to work with academics, helping them reframe their work in ways that make sense and have relevance to wider publics. Commercial organizations, like Kudos[1] have sprung up which, often with the encouragement of publishers and universities, aim to help bring academic research to ever-wider audiences. Readership hits and 'likes' on many of these platforms are now openly available giving a reasonable, if not always accurate, indication of which articles attract the attention of readers. Personal blogs as well as postings on social media can also be considered as rough indicators of academic research reaching wider audiences. Overall, we are certainly in favour of all these initiatives, recognizing however the difficulties of basing firm conclusions on any one of them. Popular pieces on rubber fetishism, or the quest for the world's hottest chilli, may attract more online hits than a carefully researched article on waste recycling.

Expert impact can be measured through references in professional publications, public reports and/or participation in significant public committees and boards, advisory and regulatory agencies, and so forth. This is more likely to reflect a public recognition of expertise rather than the interest of the general

---

[1] https://www.growkudos.com.

public. Assessment criteria can be tailored to specific disciplines. In political science, for example, references to researchers in parliamentary protocols indicate whether they have something to say of relevance for the democratic governance of their country. Thus, an overview of about eighty political science professors in Sweden showed that many were never mentioned, while the top scorers were referred to more than eighty times, indicating at least a clear relevance of their work for the heart of the country's political system. In other disciplines like sociology, economics, psychology, and social policy and social work, similar indicators may be used. For these disciplines as well as for disciplines not addressing directly social or political concerns, other measurements may be more appropriate, for example, do associations and professional national journals of social workers, psychologists, and so forth refer to senior academics and departments in the discipline? The point here is that for every discipline one could identify a few simple indicators that could evaluate its influence at a relevant sector or profession. (For more on external visibility, see Bastow et al, 2014).

We are not claiming that every academic researcher must be able to demonstrate the value of his or her work in *all* of these ways, but a clearer picture of the impact of the work of different departments will emerge if all these indicators are examined together. Nor do we claim that it is easy to get all these indicators with absolute accuracy. This is not rocket science, and a high degree of precision is both unnecessary and unwanted. As we argued earlier, finding the right balance between simplicity and accuracy is important. Key to it is not to overdo it, nor to work with misleading indicators. But a government determined to counteract the current emptiness and irrelevance of social research can use indicators like these to get a reasonable picture of the contribution of different institutions, and encourage a change in researchers' priorities and attitudes. Some incentives to get individual academics and their departments to address wider concerns and audiences could be a countermeasure to the contemporary journal publication focus. Encouragement of re-orientation should not be too difficult, too time demanding or too controversial even if, as with all evaluations, there are going to be winners and losers, and the latter are inevitably likely to seek to undermine the credibility of the indicators.

Evaluation of Research and Other Social Contributions

In this chapter we have proposed a *combination* of various indicators of meaning, relevance, and impact in social research as substitutes of current measures which are often too mechanical, encouraging instrumental and dysfunctional behaviours. We emphasize that these indicators should be applied at aggregate levels of departments and institutions, rather than become sticks with which to discipline individual researchers. A combination of these indicators would provide governments with sound information for resource allocation. Institutions that can demonstrate evidence of research which combines scientific *and* social value should then receive more funding. Within institutions, such indicators would also provide a fair insight into the contributions of different research groups and departments.

We also emphasize the need to ensure that those who lose out in the proposed new assessment regimes should not be excluded from future opportunities to enhance their performance, let alone feel shamed or disgraced. Finding different niches other than research in which to offer a useful service to their communities and their constituencies and being properly recognized and rewarded for such service is every bit as important as seeking to compete in a field which does not accord with the strengths and the talents of their faculty. In terms of governance it is essential that the results of research assessments should be clearly and transparently communicated to universities, schools, authorities, and the wider public to ensure that they all appreciate the importance accorded to the social value and meaning of the research being evaluated. Sometimes clear exposure and symbolism may matter more than monetary effects; we see the possibility of cultural change as most vital.

We are, of course, keenly aware that any scheme to evaluate social science research in different universities will be liable to gaming and, in some cases, abuse. Some of this is the result of a fetishization of rankings and league tables in which infinitesimal differences in quality or performance translate into massive leaps in the pecking order of different institutions. For example, in the UK's 2014 REF, an overall score of 3.20 places a business school in tenth place, whereas a score of 3.00 places it in forty-second place in the league table. This prompted institutions to try climbing up the pecking order to 'declare' ever fewer academics, that is, those they could confidently claim to have four publications of 'international excellence' (3*) or 'world class' (4*). The remaining were left out of the REF and, very often and unjustly, treated as second-class citizens and given heavier teaching loads. We are of the belief that such fetishization of rankings can be avoided if the results of research evaluations give an accurate but broad picture of quality, rather than aiming to draw infinitesimal comparisons between individual institutions and departments.

Governments Supporting a Renewed Emphasis on Teaching

The purpose of our proposals on research assessments is to discourage research publications that have little real value and no social relevance beyond the narrow concerns of academic microtribes. Rather than encouraging or forcing all departments and faculty to publish, we advocate measures that would support up-to-date and socially relevant scholarship, even if, in many cases, this is aimed at providing a better service to students. Higher education would benefit greatly if many more academics accepted teaching as the core of their profession, spent more time enhancing their students' learning, and used their time to read widely and critically broadening their intellectual horizons, rather than adding to the over-production of research papers. Mass education does not have to mean mass research. There is a long-standing idea that research-based teaching calls for all academics who deliver teaching to also be actively doing research themselves. Trying to maintain the Humboldtian ideal of the unity of teaching and research at a time of mass education leads to many of the problems we discussed in Part I of this book. In today's circumstances, it is better in most cases that lecturers who deliver the teaching read and follow research, participate in reading groups and seminars, and show active interest in knowledge issues without necessarily carrying out active research themselves.

An upgrading of teaching calls for substantive reforms. We do not advocate the routine promotion of academics purely on the basis of teaching qualifications or student evaluations. This would be counterproductive and promote instrumentalism and careerism. Creating an expectation of promotion across the board based on short-term teaching accomplishments would be as pointless as promoting everyone on the back of a few starred publications. But if teaching is to be properly valorized, it must be properly evaluated, praised, and rewarded. There is evidence that some governments are already looking seriously at measures to improve teaching quality. These include student evaluations, but also other indicators of accomplished teaching such as reports by external assessors, the career success of graduates, and comparative evaluations of coursework and examination results across different universities and departments. Generic cognitive tests indicating a capacity for analytical and critical thinking may also be administered to students comparing their levels of aptitude at the start and the conclusion of their studies, in order to demonstrate a department's ability to intellectually develop its students (Arum & Roksa 2011). In the UK, a wide-ranging consultation is already in place aimed at complementing the Research Excellence Framework with a Teaching Excellence Framework (UK Government Department of Education, 2016). This initiative aims to:

- ensure all students receive an excellent teaching experience that encourages original thinking, drives up engagement, and prepares them for the world of work;
- *build a culture where teaching has equal status with research*, with great teachers enjoying the same professional recognition and opportunities for career and pay progression as great researchers;

- provide students with the information they need to judge teaching quality;
- recognize institutions that do the most to welcome students from a range of backgrounds and support their retention and progression;
- include a clear set of outcome-focussed criteria and metrics.

This and similar initiatives can be interpreted as adding pressures on academics, and potentially distracting them from research activities. There are other risks too. Consumerist students in post-affluent society wanting to be spoonfed may not be the best people to assess what is good education, so 'an excellent teaching experience' may be a dubious objective. Students and graduates are notoriously unwilling to criticize or low-score their own institutions, since this would downgrade the value of their qualifications. Institutions, for their part, may use all kinds of direct and indirect pressure on their graduates to boost their responses to evaluation questionnaires. Like all evaluation schemes, this too may be liable to gaming. In spite of such reservations, however, it is our belief that, if properly administered, evaluation of the quality of instruction will enhance the profile of teaching, and offer recognition to institutions and individuals whose social contributions lie predominantly in education rather than research.

In addition to government policies, certification bodies like those accrediting professional and management degrees can play a big part in restoring teaching as a core activity for academics. There is evidence that some of these bodies like the European Foundation for Management Development (EFMD) which runs the European Quality Improvement System (EQUIS), and includes among its members the deans of most European Management and Business Schools, are deeply concerned about the effects of the unbridled emphasis on starred publications. The time may be approaching when a renewed emphasis on teaching assumes centre-stage in the policies of these bodies. Given so much research and so many writings, it makes more sense to read and use this rather than just expand the body of studies and texts read and used by fewer and fewer people.

In Conclusion

This chapter has emphasized the need for policies aimed at restoring meaning at the heart of social research. Governments cannot dictate how or to what ends research is undertaken, but they can exercise considerable influence through the policies they adopt. Government policies on resource allocation and regulation can backfire, leading to waste, red tape, and strife. But, given careful consideration, government policies can encourage institutions and individual researchers to embrace a wider social agenda in their research efforts beyond the narrow expediencies of journal publications. In this chapter we made various proposals on how to evaluate the research contributions of different faculties, schools, and departments, emphasizing the need to deploy both qualitative and quantitative criteria that recognize the social value and meaning of these contributions. We argued that indicators of research excellence should not be limited to how academics themselves define it, but should involve multiple stakeholders from different professional groups and the wider public. A diversity of assessments undertaken by diverse constituencies would counteract academic tunnel visioning.

Due to the structural forces surrounding academia and the perversions that any audit system will generate (cf. Power, 1996), we do not proclaim this to be a panacea for all academic ills. If we compare with the British REF-system that is currently under much debate, some of its problems would probably persist. As Professor of History Derek Sayer forcefully argues in *Rank Hypocrisies*, part of the irrationality of REF is that it costs so much and showers an incredible amount of work on its panellists. In the *Times Higher Education*, an anonymous panellist explained why she or he decided to quit after being instructed to 'review' seventy-five books and 360 articles for the 2014 exercise (Anonymous, 2015b). Part of what we have suggested here—to concentrate the assessments on very few publications—would remedy some of this, but not everything. For instance, Sayer contends that 'the REF is tailor-made for the self-replication and legitimation of established hierarchies and networks' (Sayer, 2014, p. 102) notably the Oxbridge and London 'golden triangle', and the Russell Group. To construct a system of panel evaluation without preferential treatment, partisanship, and inert reproduction of current elites is, particularly in smaller countries, an intricate task.

Notwithstanding, our proposals would underscore a firm norm that academic research should have something meaningful to say to broad audiences. A substantial part of it should be concerned with the main challenges of contemporary life, including economic issues, quality of working life, social inclusion, and social welfare. Policy changes must also aim to redress the balance between the claims of research with those of teaching and education, recognizing and rewarding the real contributions of the latter. The need to improve the quality of learning offered to students demands a reduction in the explosion of meaningless, esoteric, and irrelevant research activities. Many academics should write less and read more. Research should not be seen as a right or duty for all, but as an option for those with the ability, energy, and interest to do high-quality research that has something to say. This calls for a serious reduction of the overproduction of meaningless papers that steal time and attention from supporting students, reading important works, including what was published some time ago. This may seem unfair, but meaningful social research should not be an issue of maximizing employees' rights or privileges, nor of improving universities' performance statistics. Union perspectives on university life have their role, but our task in this book is to increase the value of social science for citizens, not for academics wanting promotion, a limited teaching load, or a comfortable work situation. In most cases academics should also think more about their lectures and seminars and responsibility for students, and for raising knowledge and intellectual ability. The finding of Arum and Roksa (2011) that 40 per cent of all US students do not benefit intellectually from their studies is a strong warning signal. Less single-minded focus on research and more emphasis on teaching would improve the overall functioning of many institutions in terms of their contribution to society at large. Such a change is easier said than done, but we have pointed out some of the ways in which this can be accomplished. Some 'square' measures cannot be avoided, and some imperfect indicators are probably necessary as long as neo-liberalism reigns supreme. The key point here is less about funding per se than the signalling effect and its cultural consequences for affecting thinking and values, so that more socially responsible academics take the meaning of research and the centrality of good education more seriously than is common today.

9

Conclusion

Are not most researchers committed to social relevance and improvements? Well, some are, others perhaps less so. Some are even too interested in being 'useful'. In many cases social relevance becomes a matter of satisfying the interests of an elite sponsoring research, for example, a corporate management eager to reduce competition or an interest group wanting more attention and resources to its cause. Our emphasis on social relevance aims to address broader social issues, not immediate social engineering concerns or sectional political interests. The distinction is hard to make in some cases, but the proposals contained in this book seek to disengage social science researchers from those immediately interested in specific outcomes, and engage them in the intellectual exploration of key social issues.

In this book we do not address social activism, consultancy projects, or action research. Even those who are committed to broader social concerns and the development of knowledge for the broader social good (whatever that exactly is) can easily lose their moral compass, and succumb to careerist recipes and the seductions that follow a few successes in the publishing game. Or they can become narcissistically absorbed within their own micro-universe shared by members of microtribes, but not necessarily by anyone else. Thereafter, meaning and social relevance fades from the agenda. As two of our own colleagues in economics told us:

> Most people start in their field because they are interested in social issues. But often they get very much into models and techniques and the skilful use and wish to exploit them and then gain the upper hand.

> Nobody in my department really reads anything that others [at the department] are writing. People are too specialized, don't understand much of what others are doing and reading their papers takes too much time. We look at each other's Google citations scores and compare.

A research student said that she was able to work with a PhD in economics because she liked to solve crosswords—interesting, but not really meaningful.

In response to these trends, there has emerged in economics a movement urging 'post-autistic' work, complaining that mainstream economics has become an 'autistic science', lost in 'imaginary worlds', being socially irresponsible, and being obsessed with mathematics treating this as an end in itself (Fullbrook, 2003).

We are not claiming that this is the only or best way of representing all current research in economics, but note that such complaints echo throughout social science where 'academics retreat into narrow specialisms' (Giroux, 2006, p. 64), where they address 'very limited audiences and in a language that is overly abstract, highly aestheticized, rarely takes an overt political position, and seems mostly indifferent to broader public issues' (p. 64). Strong emphasis on the quantitative performance has led to outcome productivity, but also to many dysfunctional effects including 'tunnel vision, measure fixation, sub-optimisation and pigeonholing', as Frost and Brockmann (2014) found in their study of German senior academics. In our own fields, management and sociology, critical voices claiming that we have reached a saturation state of research are constantly heard.

At its 2016 conference, the European Academy of Management dedicated most of its plenary sessions and its Presidential Board's activity to discussions on how to put an end to this situation, which was widely seen as dysfunctional and counterproductive. Many criticisms of the existing system were aired by eminent academics as well as influential deans. These included:

1. a disregard of good research published in lesser journals;
2. technically brilliant but narrow focus of research publications;
3. over-emphasis on theory at the expense of social relevance;
4. global mimicry of American standards;
5. decline of books and monographs;
6. questionable publishing practices aimed at boosting impact factors;
7. low inter-disciplinary work.

What was remarkable about these discussions was a flurry of warnings on how unsustainable the current system has become. Many eminent contributors had no hesitation in claiming that management education and research are in profound crisis. This crisis is financial with the prospect of some business schools folding in the near future, but it is also a crisis of legitimacy threatening the entire edifice of management education and research. Both governments and accrediting bodies are now concerned about the dysfunctional consequences of the publishing game on education and learning.

Part I of this book offered an analysis of the causes of what we view as a serious problem in social science, and Part II offered a number of proposals aimed at recovering meaning for the work that social science researchers do. There is currently a wealth of critique and complaints about social science research, including the sufferings of academics, and the ill effects of New

Public Management, neo-liberalism and managerialism, and the dearth of constructive proposals. Such proposals are often met with scepticism and objections, reflecting the different circumstances and anxieties that prevail in different countries and different disciplines. Our aim in this book is not to promote a centrally driven wholesale reform of the system. Such an approach would be doomed and pointless. Instead, we seek to make academics, senior administrators, and policy-makers more aware of the impasse we have reached, and to initiate a series of small-wins that will lead to changing mindsets, professional habits, and research practices. We recognize the size of the task but are concerned that complaints and criticisms alone will not lead to any substantive change. Often we fear they only lead to cynicism and defeatism and become excuses for academic narcissism and careerism. There is a surplus of complaints about government initiatives like the REF, university administrations, journal practices, the publishing game, and so forth, and we confess that we have participated in this ourselves, so we are not pointing fingers. We believe that the time is now ripe to try to recover meaning for social science research rather than add to the litanies of the system's many failings.

In concluding this book, we address some possible objections that readers may raise, by adopting the perspective of a sympathetic but critical reviewer, and we examine how we can move on.

Objection 1.   Meaning is highly subjective and hence impossible to discuss rationally and even less to evaluate objectively.

We recognize that what are meaningful practices and products to some may well not be very meaningful to others. We also recognize that late capitalist societies face constant disruptions in meaning systems, a plurality of values, and the tendency of meaning to be lost in the overabundance of information and noise. Finally, we recognize that the meaning and value of academic research can take a long time to register. What we have consistently criticized in this book, and sought to counter, is a tacit or even cynical acceptance of a state of affairs that abandons all attempt at meaningful inquiry. Also assessments of what is true, valid, rigorous, and a theoretical contribution are often contested issues. So meaning cannot be bypassed due to its extreme subjectivity, nor can other aspects of research likely to trigger diverse responses and opinions. Our proposals are aimed at restoring the quest for meaningful research in the thinking and practice of academics and discouraging the pursuit of over-specialized, tribal, and patently empty inquiry. To this end, we have advocated that the products of academic research are tested by wider audiences and stakeholders, seeking at least partial validation of its wider social significance and meaning. Meaning is not something to be settled once and for all and full consensus may be rare, but it can be placed on the agenda for reflection and communication. The *'so what'* question could be a standing issue at academic seminars, and call for as much or more discussion than issues around literature review, sample size, and data management concerns and what exactly is 'theory', and what is a sufficient theoretical contribution.

Objection 2. You place too much emphasis on individual researchers to produce meaningful research against all the pressures resulting from mass higher education and neo-liberal agendas.

We recognize that there are limits to what individual researchers can accomplish. We also recognize that not all researchers participate in the current system from the same position of privilege and power. There is no inclusive 'we' that can innocently invoke the belief that a cohesive community of scholars will debate our proposals and move on. We do claim, however, that most researchers have more power than they realize. They largely evaluate each other's efforts, they deploy resources, they promote and discourage different practices. Most academic institutions, including universities and their departments, journals, funding bodies, and advisory boards are still run by academics who wield considerable power in spite of frequent claims to the contrary. Few groups have as much individual and collective autonomy, free time, and self-governance as academics. Few groups can escape system imperatives and rigid control as easily as academics. Academic institutions, we believe, can still provide terrains from which the pressures of corporatization and neo-liberal agendas can be opposed and resisted, provided that academics as individuals, groups, and communities abandon their quiescent and conformist attitudes and their individualistic and careerist preoccupations.

The popularity of blaming 'systems' for the sad state of things is, as we see it, not only problematic because it gives a misleading account, but also because it legitimizes cynicism, opportunism, and the retreat from taking responsibility for doing meaningful work. Many academics have half their work time free for doing research, so surely it must be possible for many to produce some academically good and socially relevant studies. Failing this, we would urge them to refocus their scholarship away from research towards teaching, public engagement, curriculum development, and academic citizenship. Systems-blaming is often used to explain away one's own shortcomings as a researcher, preserving a false self-understanding about how creative, rich, and interesting one would be if it were not just for these deans, REFs, journals, editors, reviewers, and other representatives of the evil empire. While there are plenty of examples of mechanical performance control and formulaic norms for journal publication these do not pre-empt possibilities for creative and meaningful research.

Objection 3. It is easy for you who have secure appointments and established careers to preach to others. Those still struggling in the academic precariat cannot afford the luxury of thinking about these things.

As we mentioned above, we recognize that not all academics operate from the same positions of power and privilege. We would not indeed expect those most vulnerable and exposed among our colleagues to take the lead in the struggle to recover meaning for social science research, hence we see it as our responsibility to speak out from our relatively secure positions. And one cannot push for academic ideals and responsibilities through adaptation to norms appropriate for the most vulnerable and exposed. The point of research is to contribute to social knowledge, and this is demanding and calls for a reasonably high level of ability, dedication, and hard work. A university is not a social welfare institution. We cannot accept research of low quality or relevance only because that makes life meaningful for those who produce it. Furthermore, our proposals aim to undermine the dominance of the publishing game that creates so few winners and so many losers. We also want to see greater recognition for the work of those academics whose vocation and talents do not lie in doing social research. We believe that they can contribute in many different ways as teachers, critics, commentators, and citizens. In defending the idea of scholarship as entailing many diverse qualities and talents, we want to see all academics freed from the joyless, frustrating, and often vain pursuit of 'journal hits'. We would also like to add that having an academic job, even if not a permanent or senior one, is in many ways a privilege, compared to most other occupations. With this follows certain roles and duties, including the responsibility of saying something relevant, and not being exclusively concerned with securing employment and making a career.

Objection 4. In criticizing the quantity of published research materials you disregard the fact that publishing, even publishing low-quality research, is part of every researcher's training without which they cannot enhance their talents.

We do not forget the fact that nearly all scholars have to go through an apprenticeship period when they learn their trade. Inevitably, some of the work we all produce as part of our development can be mundane, conservative, and specialized. We also do not disregard the fact that younger researchers must often work in collaboration with their seniors before they can reliably make their own unique contributions to scholarship. But a fair question is: how much training or failed projects do people need? We have seen many scholars doing their best work during or just after their PhDs. We have not seen many academics starting to publish brilliant work after spending a number of years doing mediocre research. Even though not all projects can be expected to lead to valuable knowledge, the proportion between effort and success is alarmingly low. We—and many others we have talked with—feel that exposure to too many conference presentations often makes us cynical and depressed about what is being accomplished. What we oppose is the tendency for every conference or seminar presentation, every embryonic piece of research and every unripe set of arguments to seek a place in some journal or other. In developing their technical expertise, researchers may spend long hours on work that is valuable to them but has little meaning for others. We believe that indiscriminate publishing of such material is counterproductive to the author and damaging for academic research as a whole.

> *Objection 5.* Things were not better in the past. With international journals and strict review processes we have improved the quality of publications and thereby meaning in research. You are unfair in your critique of journals and peer review. They are far from perfect but better than the old rule of nepotism when editors published papers by members of their networks and tribes.

Possibly so. We agree that a key aspect of meaningful research is its academic quality. Social relevance can never compensate for academic quality. There are of course different views of what this is. The double-blind peer-review process, despite its flaws, is still the best option for academic quality control. But as we have pointed out, there are obvious and increasing problems. We have replaced strong local orientations with over-specialization. Instead of local tribes we now have global microtribes of narrow-minded specialists. New forms of parochialism increasingly mean research tribalism, gap-spotting, formulaic and socially 'autistic' work. Urgent reforms are needed to preserve peer reviews as central while minimizing their increasingly harmful features. It may not have been better in the past, but there were more important contributions a couple of decades ago, and it seems that more and more footnote-adding studies are done today.

> *Objection 6.* We need to have mass research in order to get some good contributions. As it is difficult to single these out in advance, some resources will inevitably be wasted. We need to accept that many research efforts do not bear fruit.

We have argued for a significant reduction of research time and efforts and a limitation of production of research publications. We acknowledge that with all reductions there is a risk that something potentially valuable occasionally gets lost. We see a greater risk that higher education and the instruction of students will suffer from excessive time, energy, and other resources being focussed on research. To repeat, extreme sub-specialization of research reduces its value as support for good teaching. We see a serious risk of academics reading less and becoming more narrow-minded, and simply bypassing classics and other important works outside their research box. The risk that our proposals will foreclose major research advances in social science is small. We spend more and more resources on social science and less and less, not only per active researcher, but also in absolute terms, seems to come out of all this in terms of valuable knowledge. We clearly face diminishing returns from social research. There seems to be a shared understanding that it is easier to point at really important work from the 1960s and 1970s than from the last two to three decades. The risk of a reduction of the army of paper-producing social researchers, leading to significant losses in terms of outstanding contributions, is something we—and probably people financing all this—can live with.

Objection 7. Your analysis is unrealistic. There are many successful players who do very well out of the publishing game. You ignore the interests vested in the current system which will oppose attempts to reform it.

Far from it. We are very aware that many profit from the current system. This includes elite institutions, successful academics, established journals and conferences, publishers, and other stakeholders in higher education. We ourselves actually do profit as comparatively successful authors, whose critical and nonmainstream orientations probably have been protected by journal publication regimes. Arguably, the current system gives a considerable advantage to those who are fluent in the English language, who have networking talents, and whose technical skills and tribal support help them advance their careers rapidly, earning both titles and substantial sums of money. Yet, it is curious how many *successful* players have become more disenchanted with the current system and its adverse effects on education and social relevance. If anything, it seems to us that the less successful players are more likely to resist change; they invest heavily in this system and make many sacrifices in the hope of raising their profile and joining the elite players. Many favour stricter, clearer rules and standards and may be frustrated by the broader and vaguer judgements that we advocate, for example, in assessing meaningful research and reaching both an academic audience and parts of the educated/professional public. We are not claiming that reforming the system and recovering meaning in social research will be easy, but we are confident that many of the successful players will be easier to win over than less successful ones.

Objection 8. You are voices in the wilderness, idealistic and detached from reality. The measures you propose are unrealistic and impractical.

This may well be the strongest criticism that a devil's advocate could raise against our arguments. It is a criticism that often belies cynicism, fatalism, and defeatism in the face of a system that seems omnipotent and omnipresent. We have already indicated that the system is *not* omnipotent—it entails many contradictions and creates dangerous points of stress that will inevitably lead to its decay, if not its dissolution. How long will governments be prepared to fund work that has little social value, in the light of ever more pressing claims on their budgets? How long will the tolerance of the voters and the public last for what increasingly appears as tribes of detached professionals fiddling while Rome is burning? How long will students and their parents endure intolerable levels of indebtedness and foreclosure, financing increasingly for non-academics' irrelevant research and poor education leading to non-existent jobs? How long will the majority of academics themselves put up with the joyless task of breathlessly chasing the next article hit while the pressures on them keep piling up? How long will they continue to accept inequalities that see some star-academics earning many times the salaries of those who carry the burdens of teaching?

We believe that we are fast approaching a tipping point where the current system begins to crumble, at least in some countries. This may not be apparent from the vantage point of elite institutions and star-academics, many of which are currently doing very well on the back of exorbitant fees and relatively cheap and precarious labour. Several scenarios could be sketched of what lies ahead. The worst one, at least from the sector's point of view, would be a collapse of higher education in several countries, analogous to the housing market collapse and the banking collapse. Online education may reinforce such a development. Numerous universities could end up closing, many others could be forced to close faculties and departments, and there could be mass redundancies across the board. The value of academic qualifications, including doctorates, could implode. The recent past offers many examples of supposedly robust social institutions rapidly losing their legitimacy as well as their financial bearings, and there are no reasons to believe that higher education institutions are immune to a similar fate.

Final Words

In this book, we have sought to highlight some of the endemic dysfunctions of higher education systems that have succumbed to the hegemony of meaningless research, and that have become detached from the societies that support them. We have demonstrated the grip that these systems exercise in social science, often with the collusion of academics themselves. Research has become tantamount to playing the publishing game effectively, a game that privileges technical virtuosity and extreme specialization, at the expense of knowledge addressing key social issues and problems. We criticized the

143

proliferation of meaningless publications, and the resulting downgrading of teaching as a less important part of scholarship.

In seeking to address this set of problems, we have given priority to research and knowledge for the public good, not for the benefit of researchers. We believe that many active researchers would welcome such a redirection of research focus which would lead to more satisfying work for them. However, our proposals are not intended to make the life of academics easier. We are aware that some academics who have built formidable career successes on the back of playing the publishing game effectively, and accumulating a wealth of hits, would lose out. We are also aware that some of the less successful players who are currently struggling in the hope of being recognized by a microtribe of like-minded researchers may also lose out, steered away from supposedly glamorous research and more towards teaching. We feel that this is a reasonable price to pay for a return to a social science that has something meaningful to contribute. Our proposals seek to restore meaning at the heart of social science research, even at a cost to some in our profession. It is our sincere hope that our efforts and our pleas will resonate with the experiences of our colleagues and peers, and will stimulate a genuine and timely movement for change.

Bibliography

Abbott, A. (2004). *Methods of Discovery: Heuristics for the Social Sciences*. New York: Norton.

Adler, N. J., & Harzing, A. (2009). 'When knowledge wins: transcending the sense and nonsense of academic rankings', *Academy of Management Learning and Education*, 8: 72–95.

Adorno, T. W. (2005 [1951]). *Minima Moralia: Reflections on a Damaged Life*. London; New York: Verso.

Alvesson, M. (2011). *Interpreting Interviews*. London: Sage.

Alvesson, M. (2013a). *The Triumph of Emptiness: The Social Limits of Grandiosity*. Oxford: Oxford University Press.

Alvesson, M. (2013b). 'Do we have something to say? From re-search to roi-search and back again', *Organization*, 20 (1): 79–90, p. 79.

Alvesson, M., & Gabriel, Y. (2013). 'Beyond formulaic research: In praise of greater diversity in organizational research and publications', *Academy of Management Learning and Education*, 12 (2): 245–63.

Alvesson, M., Hardy, C., & Harley, B. (2008). 'Reflecting on reflexivity: reappraising practice', *Journal of Management Studies*, 45: 480–501.

Alvesson, M., & Kärreman, D. (2011). *Qualitative Research and Theory Development*. London: Sage.

Alvesson, M., & Sandberg, J. (2013). *Constructing Research Questions: Doing Interesting Research*. London: Sage.

Alvesson, M., & Sandberg, J. (2014). 'Habitat and habitus: Boxed-in and box-breaking research', *Organization Studies*, 35 (7): 967–87.

Alvesson, M., & Sköldberg, K. (2009). *Reflexive Methodology*, 2nd edn. London: Sage.

Alvesson, M., & Spicer, A. (2016). '(Un)Conditional Surrender? Why do professionals willingly comply with managerialism', *Journal of Organizational Change Management*, 29 (1): 29–45.

Anonymous (2014). 'Confessions of an academic in the developing world', *Guardian*, 26 May.

Anonymous (2015a). 'My professor demands to be listed as an author on many of my papers', *Guardian*, 5 June.

Anonymous (2015b). 'Why I had to quit the research excellence framework panel', *Times Higher Education*, 19 November.

Arendt, H. (1958). *The Human Condition*. Chicago: University of Chicago Press.

Arum, R., & Roksa, J. (2011). *Academically Adrift: Limited Learning on College Campuses*. Chicago: University of Chicago Press.

Asplund, J. (1970). *Om Undran Infor Samhallet*. Lund: Argos.

Bachrach, P., & Baratz, M. (1962). 'Two faces of power', *American Political Science Review*, 56 (4): 947–52.

Ball, P. (2005). 'Computer conference welcomes gobbledegook paper, *Nature*, 434 (946).

Barker, J. (1993). 'Tightening the iron cage: concertive control in self-managing teams', *Administrative Science Quarterly*, 38 (3): 408–37.

Barley, S. R. (2016). '60th anniversary essay: ruminations on how we became a mystery house and how we might get out', *Administrative Science Quarterly*, 61 (1): 1–8.

Barthes, R. (1967/1977). 'The Death of the Author', trans. S. Heath, in S. Heath (ed.), *Image Music Text*, pp. 142–9. Glasgow: Collins.

Bartunek, J. M., Rynes, S. L., & Ireland, D. R. (2006). 'What makes management research interesting, and why does it matter?', *Academy of Management Journal*, 49: 9–15.

Basken, P. (2016). 'Can science's reproducibility crisis be reproduced?', *Chronicle of Higher Education*, 3 March.

Bastow, S., Dunleavy, P., and Tinkler, J. (2014). *The Impact of the Social Sciences*. London: Sage.

Becker, E. (1962). *The Birth and Death of Meaning*. Harmondsworth: Penguin.

Becker, H. S. (1998). *Tricks of the Trade: How to Think About Your Research While Doing It*. Chicago, IL: University of Chicago Press.

Bedeian, A. G. (2003). 'The manuscript review process: The proper roles of authors, referees, and editors', *Journal of Management Inquiry*, 12 (4): 331–8.

Begley, C. G., & Ellis, L. M. (2012). 'Drug development: Raise standards for preclinical cancer research', *Nature*, 483 (7391): 531–3.

Berg, M., & Seeber, B. (2016). *Slow Professor: Challenging the Culture of Speed in the Academy*. Toronto: University of Toronto Press.

Berger, L., Benschop, Y., & van den Brink, M. (2015). 'Practising gender when networking: The case of university–industry innovation projects', *Gender Work and Organization*, 22 (6): 556–78.

Billig, M. (2013). *Learn to Write Badly*. Cambridge: Cambridge University Press.

Bohannon, J. (2013). 'Who's afraid of peer review?', *Science*, 342 (6154): 66–7.

Bourdieu, P. (1993). *Sociology in Question* (Vol. 18). London: Sage.

Bourdieu, P. (1998). *Contre-feux: propos pour servir à la résistance contre l'invasion néo-libérale*. Paris: Liber-Raisons d'agir.

Brandist, C. (2016). 'The risks of Soviet-style managerialism in UK universities', *Times Higher Education*, 5 May 2016.

Burawoy, M. (2005). 'For public sociology', *SOZIALE WELT*, 56 (4): 347–74.

Burrell, G., & Morgan, G. (1979). *Sociological Paradigms and Organizational Analysis: Elements of the Sociology of Corporate Life*. London: Heinemann.

Butler, N., & Spoelstra, S. (2012). 'Your Excellency', *Organization*, 19 (6): 891–903.

Camerer, C. F., Dreber, A., Forsell, E., Ho, T.-H., Huber, J., & Johannesson, M. (2016). 'Evaluating replicability of laboratory experiments in economics', *Science*, 351 (6280): 1433–6.

Campbell, R., & Meadows, A. (2011). 'Scholarly journal publishing: where do we go from here?', *Learned Publishing*, 24 (3): 171–81.

Cederström, C., & Hoedemaekers, C. (2012). 'On dead dogs and unwritten jokes: Life in the university today', *Scandinavian Journal of Management*, 28 (3): 229–33.

Chang, A. C., & Li, P. (2015). 'Is economics research replicable? Sixty published papers from thirteen journals say 'usually not', *FEDS Working Paper*, 2015–83.

Clark, T., & Wright, M. (2009). 'So farewell then . . . reflections on editing the journal of management studies', *Journal of Management Studies*, 46: 1–9.

Clarke, C. A., Knights, D., & Jarvis, C. (2012). 'A labour of love? Academics in business schools', *Scandinavian Journal of Management*, 28 (1): 5–15.

Clarke, C. A., & Knights, D. (2015). 'Careering through academia: Securing identities or engaging ethical subjectivities?', *Human Relations*, 68 (12): 1865–88.

Comodromos, G., & Gough, R. (2015). 'The impact of change in the Australian higher education sector on the work–life balance of academics', Paper, Victoria University, Melbourne.

Courpasson, D., Arellano-Gault, D., Brown, A., & Lounsbury, M. (2008). 'Organization studies on the look-out? Being read, being listened to', *Organization Studies*, 29 (11): 1383–90.

Couzin-Frankel, J. (2013). 'Secretive and subjective, peer review proves resistant to study', *Science*, 341 (6152): 1331.

Currie, G., & Spyridonidis, D. (2016). 'Interpretation of multiple institutional logics on the ground: Actors' position, their agency and situational constraints in professionalized contexts', *Organization Studies*, 37: 77–98.

Czarniawska, B. (2004). *Narratives in Social Science Research*. London: Sage.

Daft, R. L., & Lewin, A. Y. (1990). 'Can organization studies begin to break out of the normal science straitjacket? An editorial essay', *Organization Science*, 1: 1–9.

Daft, R. L., & Lewin, A. Y. (2008). 'Rigor and relevance in organization studies: Idea migration and academic journal evolution', *Organization Science*, 19: 177–83.

Davis, G. F. (2015). 'Editorial essay: What is organizational research for?', *Administrative Science Quarterly*, 60 (2): 179–88.

Davis, M. S. (1971). 'That's interesting! Towards a phenomenology of sociology and a sociology of phenomenology', *Philosophy of Social Sciences*, 1: 309–44.

Delanty, G. (2005). *Social Science*. Buckingham: Open University Press.

Deutsch, F. M. (2007). 'Undoing gender', *Gender and Society*, 21 (1): 106–27.

Dimaggio, P. J., & Powell, W. W. (1983). 'The iron cage revisited: Institutional isomorphism and collective rationality in organizational fields', *American Sociological Review*, 48 (2): 147–60.

Docherty, T. (2014). *Universities at War*. London: Sage.

Edwards, J. R. (2010). 'Reconsidering theoretical progress in organizational and management research', *Organizational Research Methods*, 13: 615–19.

Edwards, M. A., & Siddhartha, R. (2016). 'Academic research in the 21st century: maintaining scientific integrity in a climate of perverse incentives and hypercompetition', *Environmental Engineering Science*, Forthcoming.

Eisenhardt, K. (1989). 'Building theories from case study research', *Academy of Management Review*, 14: 532–50.

Ellis, N. (2008). ' "What the hell is that?" The representation of professional service markets in *The Simpsons*', *Organization*, 15 (5): 705–23.

Enders, J. (2015). 'The academic arms race', in A. M. Pettigrew, E. Cornuel, & U. Hommel (eds), *The Institutional Development of Business Schools*. Oxford: Oxford University Press, pp. 155–75.

Fotaki, M. (2013). 'No woman is like a man (in academia): The masculine symbolic order and the unwanted female body', *Organization Studies*, 34 (9): 1251–75.

Foucault, M. (1980). *Power/Knowledge*. New York: Pantheon.

Frank, R., Gulovich, T., & Regan, T. (1993). 'Does studying economics inhibit cooperation?'. *Journal of Economic Perspectives*, 7: 159–71.

Frankl, V. E. (1984 [1956]). *Man's Search for Meaning: an Introduction to Logotherapy*. New York: Simon and Schuster.

Freud, S. (1927). 'The Future of an Illusion', in S. Freud (ed.), *Freud: Civilization, Society and Religion* (Vol. 12). Harmondsworth: Penguin.

Freud, S. (1930). 'Civilization and Its Discontents', in S. Freud (ed.), *Freud: Civilization, Society and Religion* (Vol. 12). Harmondsworth: Penguin.

Fromm, E. (1941/1966). *Escape from Freedom*. New York: Avon Library.

Fromm, E. (1976). *To Have or to Be?* London: Abacus.

Frost, J., & Brockmann, J. (2014). 'When qualitative productivity is equated with quantitative productivity: Scholars caught in a performance paradox', *Zeitschrift für Erziehungswissenschaften*.

Fullbrook, E. (2003). 'Introduction', in E. Fullbrook, (ed.), *The Crises in Economics: The Post-Autistic Movement*. London: Routledge.

Gabriel, Y. (2010). 'Organization studies: A space for ideas, identities and agonies', *Organization Studies*, 31 (6): 757–75.

Gabriel, Y. (2013). 'Surprises: Not just the spice of life but the source of knowledge', *Management*, 16 (5): 719–31.

Geertz, C. (1973). 'Interpretation of Culture.' New York: Basic Books.

George, G. (2014). 'From the editors: Rethinking management scholarship', *Academy of Management Journal*, 57: 1–6.

Ghoshal, S. (2005). 'Bad management theories are destroying good management practices', *Academy of Management Learning and Education*, 4 (1): 75–91.

Giddens, A. (1982). *Profiles and Critiques in Social Theory*. London: Macmillan.

Giroux, H. (2006). 'Higher education under siege: Implications for public intellectuals', *NEA Higher Education Journal*, Fall: 63–78.

Gouldner, A. W. (1957). 'Cosmopolitans and locals: Toward an analysis of latent social roles. I', *Administrative Science Quarterly*, 2 (3): 281–306.

Gouldner, A. W. (1970). *The Coming Crisis of Western Sociology*. New York: Basic Books.

Greenwood, R. (2016). 'OMT, then and now', *Journal of Management Inquiry*, 25 (1): 27–33.

Grey, C. (2010). 'Organizing studies: Publications, politics and polemic', *Organization Studies*, 31 (6): 677–94.

Grey, C., & Sinclair, A. (2006). 'Writing differently', *Organization*, 13: 443–53.

Habermas, J. (1972). *Knowledge and Human Interests*. London: Heinemann.

Handal, G. (2003). 'My classroom is my castle', *Forskerforum*, 167: 18.

Harley, D., & Acord, S. K. (2011). *Peer Review in Academic Promotion and Publishing: Its Meaning, Locus, and Future*. Berkeley, CA: University of California, Center for Studies in Higher Education.

Herbert, D. L., Barnett, A. G., Clarke, P., & Graves, N. (2013). 'On the time spent preparing grant proposals: An observational study of Australian researchers', *BMJ Open*, 3 (5): e002800.

Herbert, D. L., Barnett, A. G., & Graves, N. (2013). 'Funding: Australia's grant system wastes time', *Nature*, 495 (7441).

Hirsch, F. (1976). *The Social Limits to Growth*. Oxford: Oxford University Press.

Hirschman, A. O. (1970). *Exit, Voice, and Loyalty: Responses to Decline in Firms, Organizations, and States*. Cambridge, MA: Harvard University Press.

Hynes, J. (1998). *Publish and Perish: Three Tales of Tenure and Terror*. New York: Picador.

Ioannidis, J. P. (2005). 'Why most published research findings are false', *PLoS Med*, 2 (8): e124.

Jay, M. (1973). *The Dialectical Imagination: A History of the Frankfurt School and the Institute of Social Research, 1923–1950*. Boston: Little, Brown.

Johanson, L. M. (2007). 'Sitting in your readers' chair: Attending to your academic sensemakers', *Journal of Management Inquiry*, 16: 290–4.

Jump, P. (2015). 'Academics in the minority at more than two-thirds of UK universities', *Times Higher Education Supplement*, 3 September 2015.

Kallio, K. M., Kallio, T., Tienari, J., & Hyvönen, T. (2016). 'Ethos at stake: Performance management and academic work in universities', *Human Relations*, 69: 685–710.

Kingery, J. N., Erdley, C. A., & Marshall, K. C. (2011). 'Peer acceptance and friendship as predictors of early adolescents' adjustment across the middle school transition', *Merrill-Palmer Quarterly*, 57 (3): 215–43.

Klein, N. (2000). *No Logo*. London: Flamingo.

Knights, D., & Clarke, C. A. (2014). 'It's a bittersweet symphony, this life: Fragile academic selves and insecure identities at work', *Organization Studies*, 35 (3): 335–57.

Kuhn, T. S. (1970). *The Structure of Scientific Revolutions*. Chicago, IL: University of Chicago Press.

Kunda, G. (1992). *Engineering Culture: Control and Commitment in a High-Tech Corporation*. Philadelphia: Temple University Press.

Larivière, V., Gingras, Y., & Archambault, É. (2009). 'The decline in the concentration of citations, 1900–2007', *Journal of the American Society for Information Science and Technology*, 60 (4): 858–62.

Lawrence, P. A. (2008). 'Lost in publication: How measurement harms science', *Ethics in Science and Environmental Politics*, 31: 1–3.

Linder, S. B. (1969). *The Harried Welfare Class*. New York: Columbia University Press.

Locke, K., Golden-Biddle, K., & Feldman, M. (2008). 'Making doubt generative: Rethinking the role of doubt in the research process', *Organization Science*, 19: 907–18.

Lynd, R. S. (1939). *Knowledge for What? The Place of Social Science in American Culture*. Princeton, NJ: Princeton University Press.

Macdonald, S., & Kam, J. (2007). 'Ring a ring o' roses: Quality journals and gamesmanship in management studies', *Journal of Management Studies*, 44: 640–55.

Macdonald, S., & Kam, J. (2010). 'Counting footnotes: Citability in management studies', *Scandinavian Journal of Management*, 26: 189–203.

Marcuse, H. (1955). *Reason and Revolution: Hegel and the Rise of Social Theory*. London: Routledge.

Marcuse, H. (2005). *The New Left and the 1960s*. London: Routledge.

Marginson, S. (2006). 'Dynamics of national and global competition in higher education', *Higher Education*, 52: 1–39.

Martin, J. L. (2011). *The Explanation of Social Action*. Oxford; New York: Oxford University Press.

Marton, F. (1986). 'Phenomenography: A research approach to investigating different understandings of reality', *Journal of Thought*, 21 (3): 28–49.

Marx, G. T. (1990). 'Reflections on academic success and failure: Making it, forsaking it, reshaping it', in B. Berger (ed.), *Authors of Their Own Lives*, pp. 260–84. Berkeley, CA: University of California Press.

Marx, K. (1844/1972). 'Economic and philosophic manuscripts of 1844', in R. C. Tucker (ed.), *Marx–Engels Reader*. New York: Norton.

Milgram, S. (1974). *Obedience to Authority*. New York: Harper and Rowe.

Miller, F., Greenwood, R., & Prakash, R. (2009). 'What happened to organization theory?', *Journal of Management Inquiry*, 18: 273–9.

Mills, C. W. (1940). 'Situated actions and vocabularies of motive', *American Sociological Review*, 5 (6): 904–13.

Mills, C. W. (2000 [1959]). *The Sociological Imagination*. Oxford; New York: Oxford University Press.

Naidoo, R. (2016). 'The competition fetish in higher education: Varieties, animators and consequences', *British Journal of Sociology of Education*, 37 (1): 1–10.

Naidoo, R., & Williams, J. (2015). 'The neoliberal regime in English higher education: Charters, consumers and the erosion of the public good', *Critical Studies in Education*, 56 (2): 208–23.

OSC. (2012). 'An open, large-scale, collaborative effort to estimate the reproducibility of psychological science', *Perspectives on Psychological Science*, 7 (6): 657–60.

OSC. (2015). 'Estimating the reproducibility of psychological science', *Science*, 349 (6251).

Parker, M. (2013). 'Becoming editor: Or, pinocchio finally notices the strings', *tripleC: Communication, Capitalism and Critique. Open Access Journal for a Global Sustainable Information Society*, 11 (2): 461–74.

Paulsen, R. (2015). 'Non-work at work: Resistance or what?', *Organization*, 22 (3): 351–67.

Paulsen, R. (2017). 'Slipping into functional stupidity: The bifocality of organizational compliance', *Human Relations*, 70 (2): 185–210.

Perrow, C. (1986). 'Journaling careers', *Sociological Forum*, 1 (1): 169–77.

Pfeffer, J. (1993). 'Barriers to the advance of organizational science: Paradigm development as a dependent variable', *Academy of Management Review*, 18: 599–620.

Pfeffer, J. (2007). 'A modest proposal: How we might change the process and product of managerial research', *Academy of Management Journal*, 50 (6): 1334–45.

Pfeffer, P., & Fong, C. (2004). 'The business school "business": Some lessons from the US experience', *Journal of Management Studies*, 41 (8): 1501–20.

Phillips, M., Pullen, A., & Rhodes, C. (2014). 'Writing organization as gendered practice: Interrupting the libidinal economy', *Organization Studies*, 35 (3): 313–33.

Piereson, J. (2011). 'What is wrong with our universities?', *New Criterion*, 30 (September): 17.

Piketty, T. (2014). *Capital in the Twenty-First Century*. Cambridge, MA: Harvard University Press.

Potter, J., & Wetherell, M. (1987). *Discourse and Social Psychology: Beyond Attitudes and Behaviour*. London: Sage.

Power, M. (1996). 'Habermas and the counterfactual imagination', *Cardozo Law Review*, 17 (4/5–1): 1005.

Prichard, C. (2013). 'All the lonely papers, where do they all belong?', *Organization*, 20 (1): 143–50.

Pullen, A., & Rhodes, C. (2013). 'Parody, subversion and the politics of gender at work: The case of Futurama's "Raging Bender"', *Organization*, 20 (4): 512–33.

Richardson, L. (2000). 'Writing: A method of inquiry', in N. Denzin, & Y. Lincoln, (eds), *Handbook of Qualitative Research*, 2nd edn. Thousand Oaks: Sage.

Riesman, D., et al. (1950). *The Lonely Crowd*. Yale: Yale University Press.

Ritter, G. (2004). *The McDonaldization Thesis*. Thousand Oakes: Sage.

Rose, N., & Miller, P. (2010). 'Political power beyond the State: Problematics of government', *British Journal of Sociology*, 61 (s1): 271–303.

Rothstein, B. (2015). 'Guilty as charged? Human well-being and the unsung relevance of political science', in G. Peters, J. Pierre, & G. Stoker (eds), *The Relevance of Political Science*. New York: Palgrave Macmillan.

Ryan, S. (2012). 'Academic zombies: A failure of resistance or a means of survival?', *Australian Universities' Review* 54 (2): 3.

Salancik, G. R., & Pfeffer, J. (1978). 'A social information processing approach to job attitudes and task design', *Administrative Science Quarterly*, 23 (2): 224–53.

Sauder, M., & Espeland, W. E. (2009). 'The discipline of rankings: Tight coupling and organizational change', *American Sociological Review*, 74: 63–82.

Sayer, D. (2014). *Rank Hypocrisies: The Insult of the REF*. London: SAGE.

Schuster, J. H., & Finkelstein, M. J. (2008). *The American Faculty: The Restructuring of Academic Work and Careers*. Baltimore: Johns Hopkins University Press.

Schutz, A. (1967). *The Phenomenology of the Social World*. Evanston: Northwestern University Press.

Scott, M. B., & Lyman, S. M. (1968). 'Accounts', *American Sociological Review*, 33: 46–62.

Sennett, R. (1998). *The Corrosion of Character: The Personal Consequences of Work in the New Capitalism*. New York: W. W. Norton.

Sennett, R. (2006). *The Culture of the New Capitalism*. New Haven, CT: Yale University Press.

Siahpush, M., Jones, P. R., Singh, G. K., Timsina, L. R., & Martin, J. (2010). 'Association of availability of tobacco products with socio-economic and racial/ethnic characteristics of neighbourhoods', *Public Health*, 124 (9): 525–9.

Sievers, B. (1986). 'Beyond the surrogate of motivation', *Organization Studies, 7* (4): 335–51.

Sokal, A. (1996). 'A physicist experiments with cultural studies', *Lingua Franca,* May/ June.

Spicer, A., Alvesson, M., & Kärreman, D. (2009). 'Critical performativity: The unfinished business of critical management studies', *Human Relations,* 62: 537–60.

Standing, G. (2011). *The Precariat: The New Dangerous Class.* London: Bloomsbury Academic.

Stern, L. N. (2016). 'Building on success and learning from experience: An independent review of the Research Excellence Framework', https://www.gov.uk/government/uploads/system/uploads/attachment_data/file/541338/ind-16-9-ref-stern-review.pdf: HMSO.

STM. (2010). *Scientific Technical and Medical (STM) Journal Publishing in 2010.* The Hague: International Association of Scientific, Technical and Medical Publishers.

Strydom, P. (1999). 'Hermeneutic culturalism and its double. A key problem in the reflexive modernization debate', *European Journal of Social Theory,* 2: 45–59.

Svolik, M. W. (2013). 'Contracting on violence: The moral hazard in authoritarian repression and military intervention in politics', *Journal of Conflict Resolution,* 57 (5): 765–94.

Swedberg, R. (2012). 'Theorizing in sociology and social science: Turning to the context of discovery', *Theory and Society,* 41 (1): 1–40.

Sykes, G. M., & Matza, D. (1957). 'Techniques of neutralization: A theory of delinquency', *American Sociological Review,* 22: 664–70.

Taylor, M. (2012). 'It's not academic: How publishers are squelching science communication', *Discover Magazine,* 21 February.

Tourish, D., & Willmott, H. (2015). 'In defiance of folly: Journal rankings, mindless measures and the ABS guide', *Critical Perspectives on Accounting,* 26: 37–46.

Townsend, P. (1979). *Poverty in the United Kingdom: A Survey of Household Resources and Standards of Living.* Berkeley, CA: University of California Press.

Turner, S. (2007). 'Public sociology and democratic theory', *Sociology,* 41 (5): 785–98.

UK Government Department of Education. (2016). 'Teaching Excellence Framework: year 2—technical consultation', retrieved from: https://www.gov.uk/government/consultations/teaching-excellence-framework-year-2-technical-consultation.

Van Knippenberg, D., & Sitkin, S. B. (2013). 'A critical assessment of charismatic-transformational leadership research: Back to the drawing board?', *Academy of Management Annals,* 7: 1–60.

Van Maanen, J. (1988). *Tales of the Field.* Chicago, IL: University of Chicago Press.

Van Maanen, J. (1995). 'Fear and loathing in organization studies', *Organization Science,* 6 (6): 687–92.

Van Noorden, R. (2014). 'Publishers withdraw more than 120 gibberish papers', *Nature,* 24: February.

Weber, M. (1946). *From Max Weber: Essays in Sociology,* trans. H. H. Gerth and C. W. Mills. London: Routledge and Kegan Paul.

Weber, M. (1978 [1922]). *Economy and Society: An Outline of Interpretive Sociology.* Berkeley: University of California Press.

Weick, K. E. (1989). 'Theory construction as disciplined imagination', *Academy of Management Review*, 14: 516–31.

Weick, K. E. (1995). *Sensemaking in Organizations*. London: Sage.

Wellington, J., & Nixon, J. (2005). 'Shaping the field: The role of academic journal editors in the construction of education as a field of study', *British Journal of Sociology of Education*, 26 (5): 643–55.

West, C., & Zimmerman, D. H. (1987). 'Doing gender', *Gender and Society*, 1: 125–51.

Widerberg, K. (2014). 'Gränsliv', in G. Andersson, T. Brante, & C. Edling (eds), *Det personliga är sociologiskt*. Falun: Liber.

Wilkinson, R., & Pickett, K. (2010). *The Spirit Level: Why Equality is Better for Everyone*, 2nd edn. New York: Bloomsbury Press/Penguin Books.

Williams, J. E. (1965). *Stoner*. New York: New York Review Books.

Willmott, H. (2011). 'Journal list fetishism and the perversion of scholarship: Reactivity and the ABS list', *Organization*, 18 (4): 429–42.

Wilner, P. (1985). 'The main drift of sociology between 1936 and 1982', *History of Sociology*, 5 (2): 1–20.

Wolf, A. (2004). 'Education and economic performance: Simplistic theories and their policy consequences', *Oxford Review of Economic Policy*, 20 (2): 315–3.

Index

Index